Putin's Wars and NATO's Flaws

By the same author

Pen and Sword
Axis of Evil: The War on Terror Edited with Gwyn Winfield (2005).
The Rhodesian War: A Military History (with Dr Peter McLaughlin) (2008)
Mugabe's War Machine (2011).
Total Destruction of the Tamil Tigers: The Rare Victory of Sri Lanka's Long War (2012).
Omar al-Bashir and Africa's Longest War (2015)
The Jihadist Threat: The Re-conquest of Europe? (2015)
Dying for the Truth: The Concise History of Frontline War Reporting (2016)
Superpowers, Rogue States and Terrorism: Countering the Security Threats to the West (2017)
Total Onslaught: War and Revolution in Southern Africa Since 1945 (2018)
Deadlines on the Front Line: Travels with a Veteran War Correspondent (2018)
North Korea: Warring with the World (2020)
Churchill's German Special Forces (2023)

Other non-fiction
A Short Thousand Years: The End of Rhodesia's Rebellion (College Press, 1979)
Stander: Bank Robber with Mike Cohen (Galago, 1984)
Inside the Danger Zones: Travels to Arresting Places (Biteback, 2010)
Shooting the Messenger: The Politics of War Reporting with Professor Phil Taylor (Potomac, 2008, updated paperback, Biteback, 2011)
It Just Doesn't Add Up: Explaining Dyscalculia and Overcoming Number Problems for Children and Adults (Tarquin, St Albans, 2015)

Fiction
Anchoress of Shere (Poisoned Pen Press, 2002)
Regression (Millstream, 2012)

Putin's Wars and NATO's Flaws

Why Russia Invaded Ukraine

Paul Moorcraft

Pen & Sword
MILITARY

First published in Great Britain in 2023 by
Pen & Sword Military
An imprint of
Pen & Sword Books Ltd
Yorkshire – Philadelphia

Copyright © Paul Moorcraft 2023

ISBN 978 1 39903 142 4

The right of Paul Moorcraft to be identified as Author of this work has been asserted by him in accordance with the Copyright, Designs and Patents Act 1988.

A CIP catalogue record for this book is available from the British Library.

All rights reserved. No part of this book may be reproduced or transmitted in any form or by any means, electronic or mechanical including photocopying, recording or by any information storage and retrieval system, without permission from the Publisher in writing.

Typeset by Mac Style
Printed in the UK by CPI Group (UK) Ltd, Croydon, CR0 4YY.

Pen & Sword Books Limited incorporates the imprints of Atlas, Archaeology, Aviation, Discovery, Family History, Fiction, History, Maritime, Military, Military Classics, Politics, Select, Transport, True Crime, Air World, Frontline Publishing, Leo Cooper, Remember When, Seaforth Publishing, The Praetorian Press, Wharncliffe Local History, Wharncliffe Transport, Wharncliffe True Crime, White Owl and After the Battle.

For a complete list of Pen & Sword titles please contact

PEN & SWORD BOOKS LIMITED
47 Church Street, Barnsley, South Yorkshire, S70 2AS, England
E-mail: enquiries@pen-and-sword.co.uk
Website: www.pen-and-sword.co.uk

Or

PEN AND SWORD BOOKS
1950 Lawrence Rd, Havertown, PA 19083, USA
E-mail: Uspen-and-sword@casematepublishers.com
Website: www.penandswordbooks.com

Contents

Maps	vii
Timeline of Major Events in this Book	xi
Abbreviations	xxi
Glossary	xxiii
About the Author	xxv
Acknowledgements	xxvi
Introduction	xxvii
Chapter 1 Are Russians different?	1
Chapter 2 Understanding Russia: Why Putin Invaded Ukraine	7
Chapter 3 A Man Called Volodymyr	27
Chapter 4 A Man Called Vladimir	34
Chapter 5 Putin's Wars	48
Chapter 6 The Blame Game	62
Chapter 7 The Road to War	70
Chapter 8 The Russian Invasion of Ukraine	79
Chapter 9 The Wagner Mutiny	91
Chapter 10 The Role of Sanctions	102
Chapter 11 Information Warfare and Propaganda	107
Chapter 12 Give Peace a Chance?	118

Chapter 13	Give War a Chance	125
Chapter 14	A New Era?	145
Chapter 15	Conclusion	149

Appendix 1: The Blame Game Again — 157
Appendix 2: Rebuilding Ukraine — 164
Appendix 3: NATO's Expansion — 169
Appendix 4: How Likely is the Chance of the Ukraine-Russian War Going Nuclear? — 174
Notes — 177
Select Bibliography (in English) — 181
Index — 183

Maps

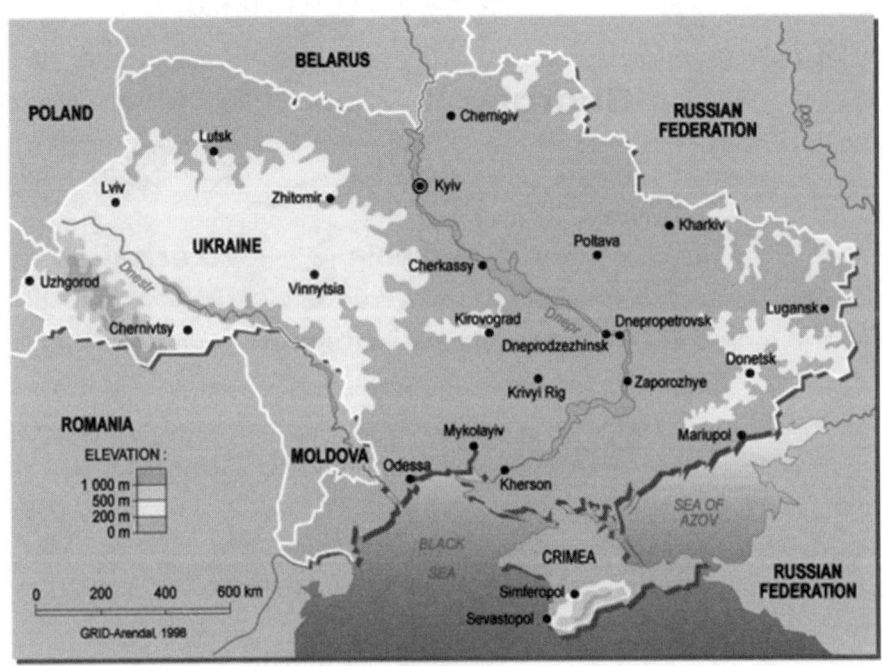

Ukraine political map. (*GRID-Arendal, CC BY-NC-SA 2.0*)

Chechnya and Caucasus. (*Kbh3rd via Wikimedia Commons, CC BY-SA 3.0*)

viii   *Putin's Wars and NATO's Flaws*

Georgia, Ossetia, Russia and Abkhazia. (*Ssolbergj via Wikimedia Commons, CC BY-SA 3.0*)

Ukraine front line Christmas 2022.

Front line August 2023.

x *Putin's Wars and NATO's Flaws*

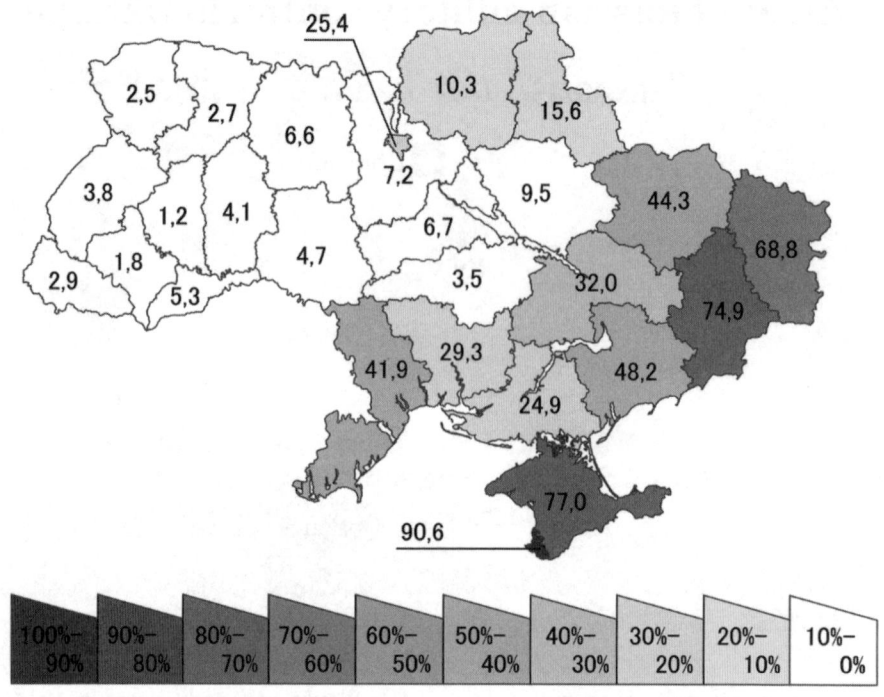

Native-born Russian speakers in Ukraine. (*Alex Tora via Wikimedia Commons, CC BY-SA 3.0*)

Timeline of Major Events in this Book

Yeltsin era

1991 – Russia becomes independent as the Soviet Union collapses and, together with Ukraine and Belarus, forms the Commonwealth of Independent States, which is eventually joined by most former Soviet republics except the Baltic states.

Chechnya declares unilateral independence, beginning a decade of conflict with Moscow.

1992 – Russia takes up the seat of the former Soviet Union on the United Nations Security Council and retains control of its nuclear arsenal.
Acting Prime Minister Yegor Gaidar launches controversial programme of lifting central controls on economy to prevent total collapse.
Opponents complain it is poorly managed and directly responsible for hyper-inflation and the rise of the 'oligarchs' – businessmen who benefit from crash privatization of massive state enterprises.

1993 – September/October – President Boris Yeltsin sends in troops to seize parliament from opponents of his rule.

1993 – December – Referendum approves new constitution giving president sweeping powers.
Communist and nationalist opposition makes large gains in elections to new Duma parliament.

1994 – Russia joins NATO's Partnership for Peace programme.
Russian troops launch two-year war to recapture the breakaway republic of Chechnya, which ends with compromise agreement on substantial Chechen autonomy.

1995 – Communist Party emerges as largest party in parliamentary elections, with more than a third of seats.

1996 – Yeltsin re-elected despite concerns about his health.
Russia admitted to the G-7 group of industrialized countries. (Suspended in March 2014.)

Yeltsin's twilight years

1998 – September – New Prime Minister Yevgeny Primakov stabilizes collapsing rouble, ends danger of debt default, and carries out major taxation reform.

Also opposes NATO campaign against Yugoslavia, marking start of Russia's distancing itself from US foreign policy. He eventually falls out with President Yeltsin, who dismisses him in May 1999.

1999 – August – Armed men from Chechnya invade the neighbouring Russian territory of Dagestan.

President Yeltsin appoints ex-KGB officer Vladimir Putin prime minister with a brief to bring Chechnya back under control.

1999 – December – Yeltsin resigns in favour of Vladimir Putin, who takes over, buoyed by popularity over major military campaign against Chechen rebels.

Putin asserts control

2000 – March – President Putin wins election.

2000 – August – Putin faces criticism over sinking of *Kursk* nuclear submarine, given his slow response and official obfuscation.

2000 – December – Mr Putin begins steady process of rehabilitating Soviet era by re-instating 1944–1991 anthem with new words.

Timeline of Major Events in this Book xiii

2002 – May – Russia and the USA announce a new agreement on strategic nuclear weapons reduction.
Russian and NATO foreign ministers set up NATO-Russia Council with equal role in decision-making on terrorism and other security threats.

2002 – October – Chechen rebels seize a Moscow theatre and hold about 800 people hostage. Most of the rebels and around 120 hostages are killed when Russian forces storm the building.

2003 – June – Government axes last remaining nationwide independent TV channel, TVS, citing financial reasons.

2003 – September – Kyrgyzstan grants Russia first military base abroad in 13 years to counter Islamist terrorism.

2003 – October – Yukos oil boss and prominent liberal Mikhail Khodorkovsky arrested on charges of tax evasion and fraud, an early casualty of President Putin's campaign to drive Yeltsin-era 'oligarchs' out of politics. In 2005 he is sentenced to nine years' imprisonment but is pardoned and goes into exile in 2013.

2003 – December – President Putin's United Russia wins landslide Duma election victory, buoyed by economic recovery.

2004 – March – Putin wins second presidential term by landslide, consolidating his power.

2004 – August – Authorities seize Yuganskneftegaz, Yukos's key production unit, over alleged tax debts, in move widely seen as punishment for Yukos boss Khodorkovsky's opposition to Putin. State formally purchases Yuganskneftegaz in December.

2004 – September – More than 380 people, many of them children, killed when mainly Chechen and Ingush Islamists besiege school in

North Ossetia's Beslan. Prompts boost in state security powers, despite widespread public criticism of handling of siege.

Putin scraps direct election of regional governors, who will henceforth be government appointees.

2005 – February – Moscow and Tehran sign agreement by which Russia will supply fuel for Iran's Bushehr nuclear reactor and Iran will send spent fuel rods back to Russia.

2005 – March – Chechen separatist leader Aslan Maskhadov killed by Russian forces.

2005 – June – State gains control of Gazprom gas giant by increasing its stake in the company to over 50 per cent.

2005 – September – Russia and Germany sign major deal to build Nord Stream gas pipeline under Baltic Sea between the two countries. Comes on line in 2011.

2006 – January – Putin signs law giving authorities extensive new powers to monitor the activities of non-governmental organisations and suspend them if they are found to pose an alleged threat to national security.

2006 – July – Russia's most-wanted man, Chechen warlord Shamil Basayev, killed by security forces.

2006 – November – Former Russian security service officer Alexander Litvinenko, an outspoken critic of the Kremlin living in exile in London, dies of polonium poisoning. Britain accuses Russian former security officers of murder.

2007 – March – Dozens detained as riot police break up St Petersburg protest by demonstrators accusing President Putin of stifling democracy.

2007 – July – Diplomatic row between London and Moscow over Britain's bid for the extradition of Andrei Lugovoi, an ex-KGB agent accused of Litvinenko's murder.

2007 – August – Russia mounts an Arctic expedition apparently aimed at expanding its territorial claims and plants a flag on the seabed at the North Pole.

2007 – November – President Putin signs law suspending Russia's participation in the 1990 Conventional Armed Forces in Europe treaty that limits the deployment of heavy military equipment across Europe.

2007 – December – President Putin's United Russia party wins landslide in parliamentary elections, which critics describe as neither free nor democratic.

2008 – January – Russia revives Soviet-era Atlantic navy exercises in neutral waters in the Bay of Biscay off France in demonstration of resurgent military muscle.

2008 – March – Putin ally Dmitry Medvedev wins presidential elections as Putin cannot serve a third consecutive term; later appoints Putin prime minister.

War with Georgia

2008 – August – Tensions with Georgia escalate into war after Georgian troops attack Russian-backed separatist forces in South Ossetia. Russia drives Georgian forces from South Ossetia and Abkhazia, then recognizes both as independent states.

2008 – November – Parliament votes overwhelmingly in favour of a bill that would extend the next president's term of office from four to six years.

2009 – January – Russia stops gas supplies to Ukraine after the collapse of talks to resolve a row over unpaid bills. Supplies to south-eastern Europe are disrupted for several weeks as a result of the dispute.

2009 – April – Russia formally ends operations against rebels in Chechnya, although sporadic violence continues.

Thaw with US

2009 – July – President Medvedev and Barack Obama, on his first official visit to Moscow, reach an outline agreement to reduce nuclear weapons stockpiles in move aimed at replacing 1991 Start 1 treaty.

2009 – September – Russia welcomes the US decision to shelve missile defence bases in Poland and the Czech Republic.

2009 – October – Opposition parties accuse the authorities of rigging local elections as the governing United Russia party wins every poll by a wide margin.

2010 – April – President Medvedev signs a new strategic arms agreement with US committing both sides to cut arsenals of deployed nuclear warheads by about 30 per cent.

2010 – June – Presidents Medvedev and Obama mark warming in ties on the Russian leader's first visit to the White House. Obama says the US will back Russia's World Trade Organization accession.

2010 – July – A customs union between Russia, Belarus and Kazakhstan comes into force despite Belarusian complaints about Russia retaining duties on oil and gas exports to its neighbours.

2010 – October – President Medvedev sacks the powerful mayor of Moscow, Yuri Luzhkov, after weeks of criticism from the Kremlin. Mayor Luzhkov had been in office since 1992.

2011 – December – United Russia suffers drop in share of the vote at parliamentary elections but keeps a simple majority in the State Duma. Tens of thousands turn out in opposition protests alleging fraud, in first major anti-government protests since the early 1990s.

Putin's second presidency

2012 – March – Putin wins presidential elections. Opponents take to the streets of several major cities to protest at the conduct of the election, police arrest hundreds.

2012 – July – Law goes into force requiring non-governmental organisations receiving funds from abroad to be classed as 'foreign agents' as part of a wider crackdown on dissent.

2012 – August – US, EU and human rights groups condemn jail sentences imposed on three members of punk band Pussy Riot over an anti-Putin protest in a Moscow cathedral. The women were sentenced to two years for 'hooliganism'.

Russia formally joins the World Trade Organization after 18 years of negotiations.

2012 – December – Angered by a US bill blacklisting Russian officials in connection with the death in custody of lawyer Sergei Magnitsky, Moscow bans Americans from adopting Russian children and stops US-funded non-governmental organisations from working in Russia.

Crackdown continues

2013 – July – Anti-corruption blogger and leading opposition activist Alexei Navalny is sentenced to five years in prison after being found guilty of embezzlement in a trial he rejects as politically motivated.

2013 – September – Navalny comes second in the Moscow mayoral election after being released pending appeal, coming close to forcing the Kremlin's candidate into a run-off.

2013 – Putin gave asylum to Edward Snowden

Ukraine crisis

2014 – February-May – After flight from Ukraine of pro-Moscow president Viktor Yanukovych, Russian forces takeover of Crimea, which then votes to join Russia in a referendum. This sparks biggest East-West showdown since Cold War, with the US and its European allies criticising Russia's further intervention in eastern Ukraine. Russia suspended from G-8 group of industrialized countries.

2014 – May – Russia's Gazprom sign 30-year deal to supply the China National Petroleum Corp with gas, estimated to be worth over $400bn.

2014 – July – Following the downing of a Malaysian Airlines passenger plane over eastern Ukraine in a suspected missile strike, Russia comes in for international criticism over supplying rebels with heavy weaponry.
The EU and US announce new sanctions against Russia. The IMF says Russian growth is slowing down to zero.

2014 – October – Russia agrees to resume gas supplies to Ukraine over the winter in a deal brokered by the EU.

2014 – December – The Russian rouble begins to drop rapidly against the US dollar, losing about half its value in the next two months.

2015 – February – Opposition activist and former first deputy prime minister Boris Nemtsov is shot dead in Moscow. Police charge two Chechens with murder amid widespread scepticism.

Syria intervention

2015 – September – Russia carries out first air strikes in Syria, saying it targets the Islamic State group. But West and Syrian opposition say it overwhelmingly targets anti-Assad rebels instead.

2015 – November – Turkey shoots down Russian warplane on Syria bombing mission. Russia, Turkey's second-largest trading partner, imposes economic sanctions.

2016 – January – British public inquiry concludes Putin probably approved murder of former Russian intelligence officer and Kremlin critic Alexander Litvinenko in London in 2006.

2016 – September – Parliamentary elections: the ruling United Russia party increases its majority, with the remaining seats won by other pro-Putin parties. Key opposition figures such as Alexei Navalny barred from standing.

2017 – April – A bomb attack on the St Petersburg metro rail system kills 13 people.

2017 – June – EU extends sanctions against Russia for another six months over the conflict in eastern Ukraine.

2017 – July-September – The US and Russia engage in a tit-for-tat involving hundreds of diplomatic staff after US Congress approved new sanctions for Russia's alleged meddling in the 2016 presidential election.

2017 – December – The International Olympic Committee bans Russia from competing in the 2018 Winter Olympics.

2018 – March – Diplomatic row with Britain over the poisoning of former spy Sergei Skripal and his daughter Yulia in Salisbury, which Britain pins firmly on Russia. British allies join London in imposing further sanctions on Russia, including the United States in August.

Putin end-game

2018 – May – Putin inaugurated for fourth term as president after beating minor candidates in the March election.

2018 – July – Putin and his US counterpart Donald Trump play down reports of Russian meddling in the 2016 US presidential election at their summit meeting in Helsinki.

2019 – April – President Putin gives North Korean leader Kim Jong-un support for security guarantees ahead of any nuclear disarmament at a meeting in the far-eastern city of Vladivostok.

2020 – January – President Putin announces plans to change the constitution ahead of the end of his presidential term in 2024, and dismisses the government.
Former tax service chief Mikhail Mishustin appointed prime minister, succeeding Putin's long-time ally Dmitry Medvedev.

2020 – August – German doctors treating Russian opposition politician Alexei Navalny conclude that he was poisoned with a Novichok nerve agent. Navalny recovers and returns to Russia where he is given a long prison sentence.

Russo-Ukrainian war

2022 – 24 February – Full-scale invasion of Ukraine. Russia and NATO now in proxy war.

2023 – June – Ukrainian summer counter-offensive begins

2023 – July – Wagner mutiny

Abbreviations

APC	Armoured Personnel Carrier
CIA	Central Intelligence Agency
CIS	Commonwealth of Independent States
CNN	Cable Network News
DoD	Department of Defense
DPR	Donetsk People's Republic
EU	European Union
FSB	Russian Federal Security Service, main domestic security and counter-intelligence agency.
GRU	Russian military Intelligence (later known as GU).
IAEA	International Atomic Energy Agency
ICC	International Criminal Court
IMF	International Monetary Fund
JCPOA	Joint Comprehensive Plan of Action (Iran nuclear deal)
KGB	Committee for State Security – Soviet intelligence and security service.
LPR	Luhansk People's Republic
MANPAD	Man-portable air-defence systems
MAP	Membership Action Plan (NATO)
MLRS	Multiple-launch Rocket System
NED	National Endowment for Democracy
NATO	North Atlantic Treaty Organization
NCO	Non-commissioned Officer
NKVD	Stalin's secret police
OSCE	Organization for Security and Cooperation in Europe

OUN	Organization of Ukrainian Nationalists (active in Poland 1930s; USSR 1940s; and the diaspora until 1991).
RPG	Rocket-Propelled Grenade
SACEUR	Supreme Allied Commander Europe (NATO)
SAM	Surface-to-Air Missile
SBU	Security Service of Ukraine, successor to the Soviet Ukrainian KGB
START	Strategic Arms Reduction Treaty
SVR	Foreign Intelligence Service
SWIFT	Society for Worldwide Interbank Financial Telecommunication.
UPA	Ukrainian Insurgent Army; partisans who fought Nazis and Red Army (1942–52)
USSR	Union of Soviet Socialist Republics

Glossary

Banderites – Followers of OUN leader Stephan Bandera but extensively used by Russia for all supporters of Ukrainian nationalism.

Boyars – Russian nobles.

Colour Revolutions – The term used for the democratic evolutions against Moscow; Ukraine was orange.

Duma – Russian parliament.

GCHQ – General Communications HQ, intelligence centre in Cheltenham, England.

Holodomor – The famine induced by Stalin that killed five million people especially in Ukraine in the 1930s.

Little Green Men – Spetsnaz troops without insignia during occupation of Crimea and eastern Ukraine in 2014.

Maidan – Square or plaza; shorthand for Independence Square in Kyiv and the revolutionary events there un 2004, 2013 and 2014.

Maskirovka – Russian military deception or hybrid war.

Minsk Accords – Negotiated in September 2014 and February 2015 by Ukraine, Russia, France and Germany.

Nomenklatura – Soviet ruling class.

Nova Rossiya – Tsarist term for eastern and southern Ukraine revived by Putin.

Oblast – Province, a term used in Soviet and post-Soviet times.

Okhrana – Tsarist secret police.

Rada – Ukrainian parliament.

RAND – US think tank.

Rokirovka – Castling in chess but swapping president and prime minister in politics.

Samizdat – Unofficial publications in the USSR.

Siloviki – the men of power/force under Putin.
Spetsnaz – Russian army and intelligence special forces.
Vozhd – leader.

About the Author

Professor Paul Moorcraft's wide-ranging career includes working for the UK Ministry of Defence in the Balkans and Middle East and being a senior instructor at both the Royal Military Academy, Sandhurst, and the Joint Services Command and Staff College, as well as working in Whitehall. As a print and broadcast journalist, he reported from thirty war zones, often behind 'enemy lines', most notably with Jihadists during the Soviet occupation of Afghanistan and with special forces in countries as far apart as Nepal and South Africa. Recently he made six trips in Darfur, Sudan, spending time with rebel groups and separately with Sudanese government forces.

He is the author of over fifty published books (including award-winning fiction) and appears regularly on radio and TV. He is, for example, the regular UK pundit for Sky News Arabic.

He has worked in Ukraine and Syria and also faced Russian troops directly in frontline combat, including daily in Afghanistan in the mid-1980s. He studied at six universities and taught, *inter alia*, Russian security policy since 1967 full-time at ten universities internationally and in the UK Ministry of Defence. A fellow of the Royal Historical Society, he returned to his Welsh homeland in 2021.

Acknowledgements

I have tried to simplify a complex story and I hope I have not overdone the simplification, not least of the Russian and Ukrainian scripts. I have largely copied the BBC style. I have tried hard to balance the opposing arguments and no doubt I have accumulated numerous splinters in my rear for sitting on too many fences. But I do believe passionately that many of us living in the West have missed out on some major angles of the story. I have witnessed Russian atrocities at first hand and close-up so I have no illusions but there are two sides to this war.

Let me first thank Henry Wilson, the then publishing director at Pen and Sword. We have done more than a dozen books together and yet again he took a punt on me. Richard Doherty was, as ever, a great editor. Matt Jones was his usual patient self as the production manager. Jon Wilkinson again provided an imposing cover design. Charles Hewitt, the boss of Pen and Sword, intervened to provide a clear sub-title. And rightly so.

My friend Wendy Gruffydd read the initial hastily written text so *Diolch yn fawr iawn*. I talked to a large number of people but let me thank Professor Elvira Rushkareva and Professor Susan Breau. Professor Vladimir Shubin, in Moscow, helped me, despite our differing opinions. Lindsey Hilsum, of Channel Four News, was a very kind and insightful colleague, as ever. Some informants, especially in Ukraine, remain anonymous.

This is a fast-moving story so I hope readers will understand if I am proved wrong, repeatedly, even before the book reaches the bookshops. As a long-term inmate of the tough school of military history I should know better than trying to cover a war that is still red hot. Forgive me but I did my best.

Paul Moorcraft, Penarth, Bro Morgannwg, August 2023

Introduction

From the Western perspective, President Vladimir Putin's invasion of Ukraine was mad as well as bad. To many in the Kremlin, however – though not to *all* – it made sense. It was both a moral duty and a historical imperative.

As Sir Alex Younger, the former head of MI6, noted: 'Putin has gone into legacy mode almost messianic in his determination to be the president that restored Russia to greatness.' Putin saw himself perhaps as a superior version of Charles de Gaulle or perhaps Francisco Franco – a very consciously transformational figure. Whether the Russian leader can emulate Kemal Atatürk, and decolonize from a declining empire to forge a modern nation state is an underlying theme of this book.

Neither East nor West wanted a nuclear war, a Third World War, but the invasion of Ukraine in 2022 made it more likely, though certainly not inevitable.

How did these polar opposites engulf Europe, nearly eighty years after Ukraine last experienced tank battles and destruction on a vast scale? Who would have thought that Germany would be sending Panzers – via Poland, 'for old times' sake', some joked in extremely poor taste – to fight again on the rich black soil and the deep snows of Ukraine?

This book explores why this tragedy happened and how Europe can perhaps heal itself and recover.

The origins and key facts of the First Cold War have been well rehearsed. The Cuban missile crisis in October 1962 is often quoted as the time the world tottered on the brink of nuclear Armageddon. Cuba and Ukraine are not completely analogous, not least because American national security is not in play now in the way it was in 1962. The better analogy is that NATO's expansion – to Moscow – is similar to the Soviets enveloping Mexico in an anti-Washington security pact.

Between 1962 and 1991 numerous other near accidents almost brought a nuclear winter to our small vulnerable planet. The West did not realize just how paranoid the Soviets were about NATO's supposedly defensive intentions. It took some top-level Russian defectors and moles to warn the West how nervous the Kremlin really was. And often Western Intelligence officials did not help. They misread even the invasion of Czechoslovakia in 1968.

Nevertheless, an intellectual army of Kremlin-watchers emerged, as did an array of hotlines that would help avoid war by accident. Then followed a galaxy of complex arms-control-and-reduction treaties. Today nearly all the Kremlinologists have disappeared (as have the arms-control measures). Few are reading the Kremlin runes in detail and the Russian speakers in Washington and Whitehall, who understood the arcane mechanics of the Cold War, have nearly all retired or died.

It is easy to point out that these legions of Western analysts completely failed to anticipate the fall of the USSR. Today, the new rapidly recruited so-called Russian experts need to learn some modesty from their predecessors' gross failures. We also live now in an age of politicized intelligence, with security agencies pandering to their political masters and their short-term, and often increasingly social-media-driven, agendas.

Part of the problem has been the lack of focus of Western intelligence systems. British spooks certainly took their eyes off the ball. Russian influence declined and then Islamist terrorism took up a lot of intelligence energy. During the Cold War 70 per cent of London's effort in GCHQ was on the Warsaw Pact; by 2006 monitoring of Russian communications was just 4 per cent of total effort. That changed when the Crimea was annexed and President Vladimir Putin's hybrid war brought horrific poisonings to London and Salisbury.

When the West 'beat' the Soviets, not least in an arms spending competition, NATO failed to appreciate how their old enemy had been humbled. Brash young Western experts marched into Moscow to teach the Russians how to run a market economy. Their triumphalism was appalling and, in the long term, fatal to a proud country in particular and East-West relations in general.

Russia could perhaps have developed a full and productive relationship with NATO as opposed to just a temporary observer status. Even Putin talked of this in the beginning of his imperium. Moscow co-operated, for example, with America after 9/11 and donated the use of its own bases to chase down the mutual Islamist enemies, especially al-Qaeda.

Adolf Hitler detailed his plans and yet few believed initially that *Mein Kampf* was his actual manifesto. In contrast with Vladimir Putin, anyone reading his 6,000-word essay written in July 2021 on the future Russian relationship with Ukraine, could not doubt his clear imperial ambitions, no matter what NATO did or did not do after the collapse of the USSR.

By the end of the Cold War, the USSR was often dubbed 'Upper Volta with nukes'. It was simply a huge clapped-out Potemkin Village with just the military veneer of a superpower, particularly an overloaded arsenal of ancient strategic nuclear weapons. Some thought the same of the Russian Federation when Ukraine, admittedly after a great deal of Western military and intelligence back-up, appeared to humble its giant military neighbour. Putin's armed forces, despite all the money spent upgrading them, appeared to be a hollowed-out shell. So, if the Ukrainian-Russian war leads to a full-on rather than a proxy NATO-Russian conflict, another 1991 could ensue, so long as Putin eschews the red nuclear button. A defeat for Putin could lead to the Russian Federation imploding, with all the old nationalities again seeking their own independent futures, amid the attempts by the United Nations to recover the world's biggest nuclear stockpiles.

Putin has vowed publicly to enact the official Russian military doctrine that the Kremlin will use its nuclear weapons only if Russia is threatened existentially. NATO had ditched its actual use of nukes in a war-fighting role decades before, though the strategic MAD doctrine – 'mutual assured destruction' – was never actually revoked.

The famous Doomsday Clock of the *Bulletin of Atomic Scientists* shows the time to be 90 seconds short of midnight, the closest to Armageddon ever. Mainly because of the Russian invasion of Ukraine.

Putin keeps doubling down and the war keeps escalating at the time of writing. This author has covered over thirty wars and knows it is always difficult to analyse a conflict while the fighting is current. Yes, this conflict could escalate into a knee-jerk nuclear war. This book's publication is predicated on that not happening, obviously. It should be noted that nearly all wars have ended, so far, well short of planetary destruction. Often in negotiation, as in the First World War, or in stalemate – for example, the civil war in Korea. The Second World War was unusual in that it ended in total defeat for the Axis powers.

Historians tend to lump together the anti-fascist conflicts of the 1930s and 1940s – in Spain, Asia and then Eastern Europe – as *one* war. In fact, it was a series of conflicts. The same could be said today, despite the fashion for calling the authoritarian-versus-democracies contest a new Cold War. The acute tensions over Taiwan are part of a separate conflict while the numerous small conflicts in Georgia, Moldova, Crimea, Chechnya etc. are separate symptoms of the failure of Russia to decolonize. North Korean clashes are intrinsic to a civil war but it also has a legacy of the former anti-colonial struggle against Japan and now an adjunct to the China-Russia axis.

It could be argued that the wars between 1914 and 1945 were all part of one long civil war in Europe. The European Union boasted that none of its existing members had ever fought each other – it appeared that advanced European civilization had banished war on the continent. Nobody expected major war again in Europe and hence the growing assertion that Russia is somehow not European, that it is *other*, mainly Asiatic and that it had never really thrown off the 'Mongol yoke'. Despite the dazzling music and literature and other superb artistic legacies, Russia has a culture, especially a political one, that is different from the traditions in most of the NATO and EU members. Russia, with its vast land mass spanning Europe and Asia, has certainly evolved in a unique way.

This book looks at the unique heritage of Russia and, arguably, Ukraine. And how they have interacted, merged, and now both embrace an unparalleled fight for survival. Today both are fighting about their incompatible foundation myths.

Putin's Wars: NATO's Flaws then considers briefly how these countries developed during the first Cold War. It then tries to interpret the Russian view of its history: that the West expanded NATO eastwards after German unification, despite promises not to do so. The Kremlin took a very different perspective of Western intervention in Iraq, Afghanistan and Libya and the divergences continued during the wars in Syria and against the Islamic State.

The narrative then considers how two 'Vladimirs' shaped the destinies of their countries: Putin and Zelensky. Ukraine means 'periphery/borderlands'. The Ukrainian president turned West while the Russian leader turned east to China, though many would interpret the events of 2014 as a Western coup in Kyiv. It was not always so and the Soviet Union had been sometimes a good neighbour. It was not just a version of the Stockholm Syndrome. All along the old Iron Curtain, in Germany and Ukraine especially, the depth and breadth of *Ostalgie* (nostalgia for communism and the certainties of the USSR) would surprise open-minded travellers. Many in Ukraine felt strong ties with their co-religionists and fellow Russian-speakers though the current war has no doubt hardened attitudes on both sides. Perhaps 40 per cent of Ukrainians have relatives in Russia, so this is something of a fratricidal, if not a civil, war.

This book examines in some detail ways of ending the Russo-Ukrainian conflict. But to end this war, it would be helpful to define exactly what kind of war it is. It is not a classic civil war, despite the fratricidal elements, because another sovereign country has invaded another sovereign state – albeit they were once part of the same political union. So it is a war about external intervention to (allegedly) help internal ethnic communities. That is the Russian perspective and they are pioneering exponents of hybrid war. That is a technique of fighting and it is not a suitable description. There is no word for this, so I shall dub it a 'cross-breed conflict' – though I might struggle to provide a 'cross-breed peace'.

The Cuban days of October 1962 do have some things in common with the nuclear crisis sixty-plus years later. The most striking comparison is that the Western democracies once again face a revanchist Russia determined to test the resolve of the liberal world. And the Kremlin is still run by a reasonably popular autocrat with almost total control of any internal opposition. It is possibly worse today because, daily, thousands are dying and being maimed in the Ukraine.

China may possibly play a broker's role despite the pragmatic coalition with its fellow autocrat. It may not. In 1962 the untried American president, J.F. Kennedy, faced down Nikita Khrushchev, who was later defenestrated by the hard men in his own Politburo because of his 'adventurism' over Cuba. The Russian Federation's Constitution, unlike the USSR's, does not allow for such a replay with Putin. A different kind of palace coup could happen but with a hard-line military nationalist taking over. The West may therefore want Putin to survive.

The story then focuses on events in 2021 and 2022 to understand why Putin invaded. The book then analyses the war – how it has been fought.

Finally, despite the spiralling deaths and destruction how can a postbellum Europe be imagined? Forecasting futures has a long precautionary history. And yet reconstruction must eventually come, morally and materially, especially in Ukraine. And will Putin ever end up in the dock of an international criminal court, just as President Slobodan Milošević was shunted out of power and then faced trial?

Putin in the dock in 2025 is as unlikely as major European tank battles seemed possible in 2021. War is always unpredictable: that is why it is so very dangerous in the new nuclear era.

Chapter One

Are Russians different?

'Are Russians different from other Europeans?' is a question that is often asked. It is, of course, a racist question, like Afrikaners during apartheid arguing that blacks were different. But it is clear that Russians have enjoyed, or suffered under, different influences from most Western European countries.

First, the distinctive terrain is important. Russia is situated on more than one continent. The country spans the northern part of the Eurasian continent; 77 per cent is in Asia, the western 23 per cent of the country is located in Europe. European Russia occupies almost 40 per cent of the total area of Europe.

The specific traits of Russia's natural environment have been: often unproductive soil, a short growing season, an abundance of land and a small population. Distance from navigable seas and, usually, arduous land travel were the main features distinguishing Russia from Western Europe. Russia contains Europe's longest river, the Volga, and its largest lake, Ladoga. Russia is also home to the world's deepest lake, Baikal, and the country has recorded the world's lowest temperature outside the North and South Poles.

Geography is a vital influence because the country has few natural defensive barriers. The flat plains have invited centuries of invasions. It is often forgotten today that the Red Army was largely responsible for the destruction of the Wehrmacht. Tens of millions of Russian civilians and soldiers died in the Second World War. That is why, in Russia, security trumps all. So, Russians have good reasons to be paranoid about foreigners. And the burden of history is part of the famous Russian mood swings – from bloated patriotism to debilitating pessimism.

The inhabitants of Russia are quite diverse: it has many languages and cultures although Russian is often the common language.

It is often said that Russia has an unpredictable past. The origin myths are frequently juggled, just as Putin is now doing with the origins of Ukraine (little Russia) as an intrinsic part of Russia, just as Belarus (white Russia) is said to be. All belong to the same nation, argued Putin: all were part of one Russia led by the Great Russians.

Russians often talk about the 'Asiatic stuff' and blame the 'Mongol Yoke'. They often relate the Russian style of ruthless dictatorship to the heritage of Mongol rule. The Mongols ruled for only 250 years and nobody would say that the Spaniards are not Europeans because they were ruled by Muslims for much longer. Geography and foreign occupation are obviously important factors. As was the religious and cultural influence of Byzantium. The country's poverty is often noted, as is the country's feudal system but it is also important to remember that the serfs were liberated in 1861 – four years before the slaves were freed in the USA.

The Russians were often looked down on by Europeans in the period before the 1917 revolution. They were considered Asiatic others, barbarians. Russian intellectuals tended to divide into two camps on this matter – Westerners and Slavophiles. In 1881 Leo Tolstoy wrote:

> In Europe we were hangers-on and slaves. While in Asia we shall be masters. In Europe we were Tatars while in Asia we can be Europeans.

In the nineteenth century Russia became an accepted part of grand European politics, partly because of its military strength, though military inadequacies prompted the disasters of 1905 and then the revolutions in 1917. The creation of the Soviet Union, however, led to a self-imposed isolation from the Western world. This was to create, as Sheila Fitzpatrick explained, 'a kind of aggressive cultural insularity conveyed through the Soviet trademark combination of boastfulness and a sense of inferiority in dealing with the West'.[1]

Russians tend to believe that the West is interested only in the ugly things that happened in the USSR. Yes, there were lots of ugly things, from the Great Purges and the Gulags to the catastrophe of Chernobyl. The West tends to focus on negative things but also acknowledges the towering intellectual achievements of Russia in the worlds of music, ballet and literature, for example. And perhaps the Russians do have something when they talk about their soulfulness compared with the shallow materialism of the West. The claim that all classes can sit in a café and discuss, say, Pushkin has some validity. Most Russians believe they have much better family and social values than the West and look down on same-sex marriages, for example. The 1917 revolution did inspire genuine idealism, and the almost messianic zeal of world socialism was not simply communist party propaganda.

Stalin's forced industrialization and agricultural collectivization, especially in Ukraine, caused much suffering but did allow the Soviet Union to resist the Nazi invasion. And it did help the USSR to compete at some levels with the rival American superpower during the (first) Cold War. The USSR did create an effective welfare state.. The life expectancy (67) of Soviet citizens at the end of the Soviet era was almost twice that of those born at its beginning.

Many of the older generation remembered the egalitarian values of the USSR and that the brief experiments with capitalism after 1990 led to suffering and even starvation. The commander of the Northern Fleet had to ask Norwegians to supply his men with food while, in the big cities, pensioners were often forced to sell off their last prized possessions.

Mikhail Gorbachev had planned to save the USSR from itself, but he had no plans to dismember the Union. The collapse was sudden and unexpected, even for the most competent of Western Kremlinologists. As the Russian-born American anthropologist Professor Alexei Yurchak's work on the USSR described it in the title of his famous book 'Everything was forever until it was no more'. How could a superpower with the most nukes in the world, with a very powerful massive army and state security system and with 20 million communist party members suddenly commit suicide without a shot being fired in its defence? Suddenly the pre-Soviet past was all many Russians could hold on to: the old two-headed imperial eagle returned as a state symbol.

Many Russians believed that the end of the Cold War was a common victory, not a humbling defeat and did not deserve American hubris. Boris Yeltsin's foreign minister, Andrei Kozyrev, was attacked in Russia for giving away too much to the West. He said to Americans: 'It's bad enough having you people tell us what you're going to do whether we like it or not. Don't add insult to injury by also telling us that it's in our best interests to obey your orders.'

And thus the over-mighty America helped to create the dictatorship led by Putin. In March 2022 he closed down the last independent newspaper in Russia, *Novaya Gazeta*. But there is more to Russian revanchism than just Putin's desire to restore the influence of the Russian Orthodox Church, rebuild the armed forces, and take back Russian-speakers in Ukraine and Georgia, and possibly in the Baltic states.

Alexsandr Dugin

Putin was never much of an intellectual, though he is an avid (if sometimes misguided) student of Russian history. 'Putin's brain', as he is often dubbed, is Alexsandr Dugin, a political philosopher who is sometimes described as a neo-fascist. Born in 1962, he left higher education without qualifications and for a while worked as a street cleaner. (Like Yevgeny Prigozhin, who was for a while a hot-dog salesman, Dugin prospered because of his connection with Putin, though some analysts suggest that Dugin's influence has been exaggerated.) Western experts such as Mark Galeotti attacked the idea of Dugin as a latter-day Rasputin and said the philosopher had very little influence on Putin's politics. Other writers suggest that he was influential but in a more indirect way because he expressed clearly the post-Soviet angst and identified the forces of disorientation and resentment that helped to fuel Putin's actions. Dugin, however, may well have had far more influence with the Russian separatists in Ukraine.

Dugin published an influential book in 1997 called *Foundation of Geopolitics*. It was described by some US critics as being the source of Russia's 'Manifest Destiny'. Essentially he wanted to create a new Euro-Asian empire that could challenge the US-led Western world. Dugin did try to start up a number of political parties but he has achieved fame as a public intellectual who has praised Putin to the skies: 'Putin is everything. Putin is absolute and Putin is indispensable.'

Dugin published a number of tracts on why Russian renaissance could come only if Ukraine were defeated. He advocated the annexation of Crimea and then the intervention in the Donbas. Dugan could be considered as an intellectual leader of the so-called war party in the Kremlin. His daughter, Darya Dugina, was killed in a car bombing in Moscow on 20 August 2022. Ukrainians were blamed, but Dugin switched cars at the last minute, so he may well have been the target not his daughter.

Mikhail Shishkin

Shishkin is the most prominent novelist of his generation though he has lived in exile in Switzerland for eighteen years. He has a Russian father and Ukrainian mother and is an outspoken critic of Putin, especially his war in Ukraine. In his book, *Russia: War or Peace?* (published in 2023) he explains that many people in the USA and Western Europe assumed that when communism collapsed capitalism and an open society would 'return'. Shishkin argued that this idea is a complete misconception. They did not understand how deep-rooted 'unfreedom' is. It is intrinsic to his homeland and always has been. He traced Russian history from the Mongols all the way to the *Siloviki*, the men of power/force under Putin. The bosses or boss have always ruled. Nobody believed they were really free – even under the dictatorship of the proletariat individuals were the property of the state. The cult of personality around the leader (the *vozhd*) has remained the same. Russia is not littered by statues of Putin as happened with Stalin – the cult of Putin is, however, pervasive.

Nor have Westerners understood Russian economic history. The country has never had proper laws of ownership. Even today's oligarchs don't have real freedom – the state is still in control. And they know that men in uniforms can come and take their palace or boats way from them. That is one reason why the mega-rich oligarchs stashed so much money abroad. As Shishkin puts it, 'Today you're an oligarch; tomorrow you'll be lying in a cot in a prison cell.'

The exceptions to authoritarianism were few. In 1917 the Bolsheviks permitted a democratic parliament to exist for thirteen hours before closing it down for the next seventy years. Then, after 1991, there was a brief period when anything seemed possible but the instability led to a yearning for a new leader to take control. Retaking Ukraine is the beginning, not the end of Russia's rise to greatness again, according to Putin, says the novelist.

Shishkin wrote: 'In Putin's Russia it's impossible to breathe. The stench from the policeman's boot is too strong.'

It is almost to impossible to generalize about Russia because it is so varied. Moscow can be a vibrant capital like New York or London and the Federation spans so many times from frozen Archangel to steamy Sochi. Yes, Russians exhibit strong discipline and also chronic drunkenness. It's partly a problem of perception. Westerners, particularly the British, tend to think of Bond villains or, more recently, the kind of Mafia-type bosses in the popular *John Wick* series of films. Britain has produced a series of films and plays about the poisoning of Alexander Litvinenko in London and the Salisbury poisoning of a defector and his daughter, Sergei and Yulia Skripal. All this makes Russia, especially its government, and especially after the atrocities in Ukraine, as akin to Mordor. Maybe Britain and Russia are more alike, however, than they like to think: they are both bookends of Europe, and have lost their empires but have forgotten how to be mere countries.[2]

Chapter Two

Understanding Russia: Why Putin Invaded Ukraine

The most important factor in any war is to understand your enemy. Russian history can reflect nearly all the sweeping interpretations of how nations behave. It depends, however, partly on *where* you are standing – in snowbound and besieged Moscow or Washington D.C. on a balmy Sunday when the cherry blossoms are in season, for example. Is ideology important? Yes, because once upon a time communism was going to sweep the world. The great man theory has validity too or, in the case of Catherine the Great, the great *woman* theory. Sometimes they might coalesce as in Vladimir Lenin's secret journey to Petrograd's Finland Station, kindly arranged by the scheming Germans because the goatee-ed Russian revolutionary called for immediate peace with Berlin. An even older historical tradition maintains that geography shapes politics – hence geopolitics. Russia is vast, the biggest country in the world, and much of it is inaccessible and frozen. In particular, Imperial Russia suffered because of its lack of a warm-water port; old-fashioned thinking maybe but still relevant today.

To the West the Russian bear is often perceived as ferocious when not hibernating. The bear is an apt symbol of Russia – majestic, yet unpredictable when woken up. From the bear's perspective, the West has usually been aggressive. The massive barrier of Siberia in the east has protected that flank but the north European plain has afforded a convenient invasion route for the Poles, the Swedes, the French under Napoleon, and the German army – twice.

Just as one man's terrorist is another man's freedom fighter, so too Russia's defensiveness based on hard experience may be perceived by an

American general as instinctive aggression. The British Army tried to teach its new officers to understand the action-reaction cycle of modern warfare. In 1972 Peter Vigor helped to set up the Soviet Studies Research Centre at the Royal Military Academy, Sandhurst. Based on his own experiences of Russians in the Second World War, Peter would deliver a lecture as if he were addressing Soviet officer-cadets at the famous Frunze military academy in Moscow.

He would talk about the mass Russian casualties of both world wars, the abiding fear that the Western allies would forge a separate peace with the Germans. Peter would throw in the acute humiliation of the Brest-Litovsk Treaty that Berlin imposed in 1918. A reminder that the intervention in the Russian civil war was an attempt to strangle the Bolshevik revolution at birth would follow. Russians could be trusted, said Commissar Peter. Stalin kept his word to Churchill by staying out of the civil war in Greece and the Politburo pulled out of Austria as Stalin had promised before he died. Stalin also kept his promise to attack Japan within three months of the end of the war in Europe. Nevertheless, the West helped the fascist West Germans to re-arm. The Moscow-led Warsaw Pact was established six years *after* the North Atlantic Treaty Organization was founded, and only when West Germany had joined the American-dominated alliance. The CIA stirred up all sorts of revolts and sedition in peaceful Eastern Europe. Meanwhile, the imperialists waged war on many progressive Soviet allies throughout South America, Africa and Asia. Regarding Cuba, it was only Soviet good sense that prevented an all-out nuclear exchange in 1962.

Peter Vigor's chilling ventriloquism lasted till the early 1980s. A latter-day Vigor would say that Moscow showed great restraint when the (first) Cold War collapsed. Force was not used anywhere, though Soviet/Russian intelligence played a part in setting up a popular front in Romania after the gory death of one of the nastiest of the dictators, Nicolai Ceausescu. Even in the heartland of the previous world war, the Soviets withdrew from East Germany on the understanding that it would not be absorbed into NATO. They insisted that the Americans promised that the newly enfranchised countries of the Warsaw Pact would *not* join NATO. They all did, as did the Baltic states, which had been part of the USSR. Moscow was encircled by enemy troops. As Russian generals used to say, 'NATO forces in Estonia are just a short bus ride [100 miles] from St Petersburg.'

In the West, it is often forgotten that the Red Army did most of the heavy lifting in destroying Adolf Hitler, losing 20 million of its combatants and civilians in the process. Stalin saved Britain from likely defeat. The general view among Russians is that their motherland has rescued Europe from barbarism and enslavement many times: from the Mongols, Napoleon and Hitler in the past and from the Islamic State and other bloodthirsty jihadists more recently. It was only Vladimir Putin who shook the tree in Syria and kick-started the beginning of the end for the head-choppers in the so-called caliphate.

The Soviet Union, however, turned out indeed to be 'Upper Volta with nukes', a vast Potemkin village. Lenin and Co. prophesied that Western capitalism would collapse because of its own internal contradictions, yet the USSR imploded instead. Few Sovietologists in the West saw it coming, perhaps because of constant misperceptions of the Russians themselves, made more opaque by the generally closed nature of their society. It is true that Vladimir Putin had dramatically increased the defence budget but Russian military spending had been on average one-tenth of NATO's while their economy was one-twentieth, smaller than Brazil, Italy or Canada.

Maybe the West should have been nicer to the bankrupt forlorn country when it disintegrated under the drunken leadership of Boris Yeltsin. Although Russian membership of NATO was discussed, no strategic plan crystallized to bring Moscow in from the cold. Whether Russia, especially under an early Putin, would ever have joined is a moot point. Washington did not offer any kind of Marshall Plan Mark 2 or praise the country for its bloodless revolution.

Instead, Moscow was smothered by a blanket of American hubristic triumphalism. The Americans sent earnest if naïve young graduates from the Harvard Business School and the like to teach the poor benighted Russians how to privatize their industries and how to embrace the glories of capitalism.

The rise of Putin

How did the sense of closure, even the alleged 'end of history' in the early 1990s, become Cold War Mark 2, possibly more dangerous than the first version?

Putin's Russia meant a reversion to type – one-man rule, the personalization of politics. The once oligarch Boris Berezovsky, who knew Putin well, said, 'The Russian regime has no ideology, no party, no politics – it is nothing but the power of a single man.'

More liberal Russians, however, had begun to think of themselves increasingly as Europeans rather than citizens of a highly personalized kleptocracy. Putin had no belief system or civilian project to offer his people beyond revived military strength, beefed up with old-time nationalism and religious orthodoxy. This is what Stalin had done when the Germans reached the outskirts of Moscow. Yet even the fearsome Stalin had men like Marshal Georgy Zhukov who could temper his monomania. Putin did not have a politburo. He ruled alone. Putin was uniquely unilateral.

Wealthy Russians rushed to buy up smart apartments in London while their homeland retreated into a fortress Russia partly as a result of Putin's military adventures. Disputed parts of Georgia were recaptured from the Georgian army in 2008. Opponents of Putin compared this with Hitler's march into the Rhineland in the 1930s. The highly efficient grab of the Crimea and other parts of eastern Ukraine were the equivalent of Hitler's seizure of the Sudetenland. Or perhaps the comparison could be made with Britain protecting the Falkland Islanders in 1982, except that in Ukraine the compatriots were next door. It was conjectured in the West that the final move into the Baltic states would parallel the Nazi invasion of Poland that triggered the Second World War. Western sanctions were imposed on Russia, which increasingly looked east, not just to China but to forge a Eurasian customs union with some of the former Soviet Republics. The Eurasian Economic Union (EEU) was officially launched on 1 January 2015. Meanwhile, Moscow deployed its hybrid warfare – a clever mix of force and deception called *maskirovka*.

Understanding Russia: Why Putin Invaded Ukraine 11

The Western penetration of Ukraine, encouraging membership of the EU and especially NATO, was a provocation too far to the new breed of nationalists ruling in the Kremlin. Kyiv, the Ukrainian capital, had been the historic embryo of the Russian soul. That was the romantic side; more practically, the industrial regions of Ukraine contained crucial defence production facilities. Ukraine itself was an artificial construct created by various border changes (1922–54) that pushed the country hundreds of miles farther west. It did, however, gain more territory than it lost, especially to the Russian Federation in the east.

After what Putin described as a fascist coup in Ukraine, Russian intelligence stirred up insurgency in the areas heavily populated by ethnic Russians. Putin's tactics were infiltration with soldiers, usually special forces in non-Russian uniforms (nicknamed 'little green men'), plus loads of weapons, including the *Buk* anti-aircraft system that almost certainly shot down the civilian Malaysian Airlines Flight MH17. Always denying responsibility for the fighting in Ukraine with a straight face left Western governments unsure how to respond. Sending in too many weapons and trainers to the pro-Western government in Kyiv might have provoked a more overt occupation in eastern Ukraine, thus establishing a land bridge with the Crimean peninsula. Russia had the Crimean naval base of Sevastopol, formerly on lease, now part of Russia proper, and, finally, complete control of a warm-water port. (Though there were restrictions on military vessels passing through the Ankara-controlled Turkish Straits.)

If Ukraine could secede from the USSR, why can't Crimea secede from Ukraine? was Putin's logic.

The collapse of the USSR and the subsequent first war in Chechnya had demonstrated the operational deterioration of the Russian armed forces. The savage fighting against the Islamist and national causes in the Caucasus displayed the brutality and indiscipline of the ordinary Russian infantry, though the elite forces did better. In 1999 Moscow dramatically sent an armoured column to block Pristina airport as NATO forces moved into Kosovo. (This author happened to be with the British forces that first encountered them.)[1] The American General Wesley Clark had ordered the advancing Brits to destroy the column but British General

Mike Jackson refused, saying that 'I am not about to start World War Three.' Instead, the British had to feed and water the Russians.

The short 2008 war with Georgia also exposed Russian deficiencies. Putin then poured money into the defence budget, including new equipment, for example the Armata main battle tank, that was said to be the best in the world. Their operations in Ukraine and Syria indicated that Russia's forces were now perhaps somewhat more capable. They also modernized their precision-guided weapons and their command and control systems. The revitalized Russian forces had fought weak opponents in Georgia. The Ukrainian forces who fought in 2014–15 were poorly trained, ill-armed and demoralized. The Syrian rebels, both Islamist and more secular, had often fought with determination but they did not possess an air force, navy or advanced land warfare systems.

The strategic thinking in the Obama White House was channelled through the prism of Russia's ailing economy that was further enfeebled by Western sanctions and the (inevitably temporary) drop in the oil price. Putin's military bravado was perceived as a front to rally domestic support in a country going down the economic tubes. As Barack Obama put it, Putin was 'pursuing nineteenth-century policies with twentieth-century weapons in the twenty-first century'.

Russia had given up on integrating with the West; Moscow would focus on the post-Soviet Eurasia. Strategic ties with China would be built up, while Western influence would be minimized. This trend was exacerbated when general economic sanctions imposed by the EU and America were tightened to include specific companies linked to Putin's inner circle.

Tensions grew with the West over more than sanctions. In Syria both Russian and American militaries tried to manage de-confliction of aircraft. Nobody wanted accidental superpower dogfights. In Europe, aerial brinkmanship was reaching dangerous levels. Russian warplanes were constantly buzzing Western jets, both civilian and military. One of the most serious incidents happened on 7 April 2015: a Russian Su-27 (NATO designation Flanker) flew very close to an American RC-135 reconnaissance plane in international air space over the Baltic

Sea. Washington went through diplomatic and intelligence channels to complain about the highly unsafe behaviour but Moscow said the American aircraft had been flying with its identifying transponder turned off.

Shooting down of planes could have led to accidental war between Russia and NATO. Yet some co-ordination over Syria and attempted peace talks and occasional truces as well as airspace management meant that both Washington and Moscow had to talk sometimes. Even more crucially, the two adversaries continued to work on constraining Iran's nuclear aspirations. Also, Washington still needed Russian rockets, not just to send Western astronauts to the international space station, but also – it was not played up in the media – to launch American military satellites. The US would eventually build its own rockets again but it was cheaper to use Russia's ageing though reliable rockets. It suited big financial interests in both countries to maintain this eccentric connection.

Putin continued to rail against the West not just over sanctions but also for failing to stop the Islamic State and sometimes even to blame Washington for instigating Islamist opposition to President Assad of Syria. Most sensitive to the ex-KGB colonel was the threat from Europe. From Putin's historical perspective, NATO was a capitalistic tool that was starting to occupy too much of Moscow's 'near abroad'. Putin warned that sanctions were a part of

> the policy of containment ... [which] has been carried out against our country for many years, always, for decades, if not centuries. In short, whenever someone thinks that Russia has become too strong or independent, these tools are quickly put into use.

Putin deployed the 'fortress Russia' argument to bolster his own popularity. Defending the Russian people in neighbouring states, especially in Ukraine, galvanized domestic support in Russia. The return to the homeland of Crimea was especially popular among ordinary Russians. Even Gorbachev, a big critic of Putin, called it 'a happy event'. The Crimean peninsula had been formally annexed in 1783 after the hated Ottomans had been defeated in battle. It had been given to Kyiv in 1954 as a token gesture by President Khrushchev to celebrate Ukraine's integration into Russia 300 years before. The defence of Russians and Russian speakers in eastern Ukraine was a big crowd-pleaser inside Russia. According to opinion polls, not all government-sponsored, Putin's rating averaged around 85 per cent, a figure that Western politicians could only dream about. The decline in living standards, partly caused by sanctions, appeared not to influence the President's poll ratings very much. Around 14 per cent of Russians thought that the government should take measures to get them lifted. Regular majorities in polls showed that the EU and, especially, America were considered hostile and deploying a variety of propaganda and physical threats. For example, the sporting bans on Russian athletes because of doping were considered the West's own brand of hybrid warfare.

If not sending sportspeople to the Rio Olympics was a blow to Russian prestige, the geopolitical threat was still paramount. The West simply failed fully to comprehend that dangling EU membership in front of Kyiv was seen as an inevitable precursor to NATO membership. This was an existential red line for Putin. The continued eastward march of NATO was what prompted his famous warning:

> Russia found itself in a position it could not retreat from. If you compress the spring all the way to its limit, it will snap back hard. You must always remember this.

The road to full-scale war in Ukraine

From the perspective of the Kremlin, the NATO alliance was constantly provocative. The Russian president said that the Western alliance had 'replied to our security concerns by just spitting in our faces'. Putin had tried to ally with the West in the war on terror, not least because Russia had its own problems with domestic Islamism. But the anti-Jihadism of the West soon led to the invasions of Afghanistan and Iraq. The ousting of President Gaddafi of Libya was seen as a perversion of UN rules. As was the NATO invasion of Kosovo. The installation of NATO missile sites in the Czech Republic and Poland added to the image of bellicosity, at least in Putin's perspective.

It was the US meddling in Russia's 'near abroad' that really upset the Kremlin leadership. The US had its own version, after all: the Monroe doctrine. How would Washington react to Russian missiles placed in Mexico?

The Rose revolution in Georgia (2003) and the Orange Revolution in the following year in Ukraine, the alleged American meddling in the so-called Tulip Revolution in Kyrgyzstan drove Putin to a frenzy. 'If you have permanent revolutions you risk plunging the post-Soviet space into endless conflict,' he said.

Constant Western intercession in Ukraine, after endless Kremlin warnings, was the final straw for a proud man and a proud nation. 'Our Western partners have crossed a line.' He said that the people who had come to power in Kyiv were 'nationalists, Russophobes and anti-Semites'.

The invasion of Ukraine in February 2022 was savage. It was reckless and indefensible and it backfired on Putin. NATO has expanded and Putin's domestic bases, in voter popularity and economic stability, were undermined. Putin's own position was now irrevocably tied to victory in Ukraine. If he fell, that might not end the war because he was likely to be replaced by an even more militaristic revanchist.

Despite the moral case, including the many war crimes committed by the Russians, it is vital to understand why Putin did what he did. Above all, the West was seen to renege on its promises not to expand eastwards after German re-unification. Putin could not but be angered by the American manipulation of the 2014 coup in Ukraine and then Washington's backing of Kyiv's failure to implement the Minsk peace agreements.

Putin had often felt humiliated when his peace overtures were ignored or rebuffed. In 2011 the Americans had armed and trained Jihadist opposition groups, some once aligned with al-Qaeda, in the war to overthrow President Assad, a close friend of the Kremlin. Putin did manage to work with President Obama to resolve the crisis over the use of chemical weapons in Syria and they co-operated to begin the CPOA nuclear agreement with Iran.

Yet Ukraine became the sticking point that prompted the Second Cold War and then became what may be termed the crucible not only of the first major war in Europe since 1945 but perhaps the beginnings of the Third World War.

Most of what is now Ukraine had been part of the Russian empire for centuries. After the Russian revolution, various forces, including nationalists, tried to take control. It was not until 1922 that Ukraine became part of the USSR. In the Second World War some Ukrainian nationalists fought on the German side and indulged in genocide against the Jews and the Poles. The Kremlin accused the new government in 2014 of backing some neo-Nazi militias. NATO expansion was a disaster waiting to happen as some (but not enough) Western academics and diplomats predicted. 'The people of Ukraine were unwittingly caught in a perfect storm, whipped up not only by brutal Russian aggression but also by astonishing Western hubris and stupidity.'[2]

With the break-up of the USSR and Ukrainian independence in 1991, most of the Crimean peninsula was re-organized as the Republic of Crimea, although in 1995 the Republic was forcibly abolished by Ukraine with the renamed Autonomous Republic of Crimea established firmly under Ukrainian authority. A 1997 treaty partitioned the Russian Black Sea Fleet, allowing Russia to continue basing its fleet in Sevastopol, with the lease extended in 2010.

Just as in Russia, Western-inspired economic shock therapy in Ukraine helped to create runaway inflation and a 50 per cent reduction in GDP. And just as in Russia, so too in Ukraine: a corrupt group of oligarchs grabbed state-owned assets. Slowly, under the often scandal-ridden leadership of President Leonid Kuchma, the economy improved, however.

Much of the corruption centred on the 2004 election. Key runners included Viktor Yanukovych, the former governor of Donetsk who had also served as prime minister under Kuchma. Yanukovych was almost the equivalent of a mafia boss who ran the oligarchs who controlled the traditional heavy industries in the Donbas. Despite, or because of, the fact that many of these industries were rust-buckets, they were closely aligned to Russia. This is where the steel was made for the many Ukrainian versions of Soviet weapons and planes, including symbolically the famed, and feared, Mi-24 gunships. Codenamed Hind by NATO, these gunships had dominated the skies in the first years of the Russian invasion of Afghanistan.

Nevertheless, despite the close economic ties with Russia, as prime minister, Yanukovych had advocated Ukraine's membership of the EU but *not* NATO. Surprisingly, he sent Ukrainian forces to join the American-led occupation of Iraq.

Yanukovych's main opponent in the 2004 presidential election was Viktor Yushchenko, another former prime minister who had been a pro-Western governor of the Central Bank.

It was a bitter and dirty campaign in which Yushchenko was poisoned by dioxin and almost died. His face was grievously disfigured although he eventually made a full recovery. He was also accused by his main opponent of being a neo-Nazi, even though his father was a Red Army soldier who had amazingly survived Auschwitz and his mother had taken enormous risks by hiding three Jewish girls for over eighteen months during the German occupation. Yushchenko had also extensively courted the Jewish community in Ukraine.

Despite his bad health, he continued campaigning and he gained a slight lead in in the first round of voting. In the run-off, Yanukovych won a narrow, if disputed, victory. Now the country was divided between east and west in terms of ideology and of demography. Yanukovych had taken the Russian-speaking east and south, while Yushchenko had won the west and north, including Kyiv.

The Russian observers endorsed the results, while the Western organisations, especially the EU, backed Yushchenko's cries of fraud. The pro-Western groups came out in the streets of Kyiv in what became known as the Orange Revolution; Orange was the colour used in the campaign branding. The country's Supreme Court challenged the results and insisted that a new election should be held. Yushchenko won this time. The result was 52 per cent to 44 per cent.

But the victors started arguing among themselves, in true Ukrainian fashion. The new president fell out with all his cabinet and fired them all including the prime minister, Yulia Tymoshenko, who had become famous in the West as much because of her telegenic braided hairstyle as her pro-NATO and pro-EU politics. Tymoshenko became the first (and only) female Ukrainian prime minister and was premier a second time. Originally an academic economist and successful businesswoman, she had to learn to speak Ukrainian when she first entered the parliament. *Forbes* magazine named her as one of the three most powerful women in the world in 2005, although her rating dropped dramatically when she was later accused of corruption and imprisoned. She was rehabilitated after 2014.

In 2006 the struggling Yushchenko administration appointed his former bitter rival Yanukovych as his prime minister in an effort to stabilize his government and to try to heal some of the old rifts in the country. In the election of 2010, the original supporters of the Orange Revolution had become sorely disillusioned. Yushchenko secured 5 per cent of the first-time votes. In the run-off between Yanukovych and Tymoshenko the former won by a small margin leaving the same east-west demographic and linguistic fault lines.

Although Yanukovych said he wanted to join the EU, he was also determined to maintain close ties to next-door Russia. He promised that Ukraine would remain neutral when it came to security pacts. Ukraine's endemic corruption worsened under the venal rule of Yanukovych. His family became billionaires and he flaunted his wealth with a mansion on his 350-acre estate. It notoriously included a private golf course, Orthodox church, ostrich farm, equestrian centre and a museum for his many classic cars. He also became infamous for the pirate ship on the Dnieper River running through the estate. Opposition media competed in lurid descriptions of the extravagant parties held on the ship. They used to call the complex 'Yanukdisneyland'. (After his fall from power, it became a public museum and, following the 2022 war, it housed many refugees.)

Despite all the scandals, Yanukovych's Party of the Regions maintained control in the 2012 parliamentary elections. In the same election the

Svoboda (Freedom) party won 37 of the 450 parliamentary seats. Many Western observers condemned the party as neo-Nazi because of its fierce Ukrainian nationalism and anti-Russian (and sometimes anti-Semitic) rhetoric. Its support was based largely in the west of Ukraine. The rise of the right and the endemic corruption of the oligarchs added to the EU's reluctance to accept an unreformed Ukraine into the Union. The EU also condemned the political prosecution of Yulia Tymoshenko who was sentenced to seven years in jail. While EU accession stalled, the door to the Eurasian Customs Union between Russia, Belarus and Kazakhstan stood wide open.

Euromaidan

The uprising lasted three months: 21 November 2013 to 22 February 2014. It centred on the parliament reneging on an EU deal but was fundamentally about the centuries-old issue of the relationship with Russia. In a reprise of the 2004 Orange Revolution, on 21 November 2013 thousands of people filled the Maidan or main square in Kyiv. The thrust was to pressurize the government to speed up accession to the EU – hence 'Euromaidan'. The flag of the Svoboda party, with its three-finger salute, flew among many other Ukraine and EU flags. The anger at the broken promises to join the EU was palpable, as was the dissatisfaction with Yanukovych's corruption.

When police riot squads broke up the protest camp, tens of thousands of demonstrators joined the new camp on St Michael's Square. On 1 December 2013, the small army of protesters, despite the cold, stormed back into the Maidan and occupied the Kyiv city hall and other administrative buildings. Battles ensued with the riot police using stun grenades, while the protesters threw rocks and Molotov cocktails. Eventually perhaps up to half a million protesters were involved. As the protest turned more violent, some of the opposition leaders tried to stop the violence. The former world heavyweight champion boxer Vitali Klitschko said that much of the violence was caused by provocateurs.[3]

Nevertheless, semi-fascist militias, some associated with the Svoboda party, did form armed units to resist the police. One extreme group, the Right Sector, had identified with the Ukrainian Insurgent Army (UPA) that murdered tens of thousands of Jews and Poles during the Second World War. According to the tides of fighting, the UPA fought against (and allied with) both Wehrmacht and the Red Army but its prime opponents were always considered to be communists. The Red Army continued to hunt down armed UPA forces until ten years after Hitler's death.

Special forces joined the local police to break up the Maidan encampment and, on the coldest night of the winter, in the early hours of 11 December, President Yanukovych offered a 'national dialogue' while EU and American diplomats were in town but, behind the scenes, Russia dangled a generous trade deal. The violence grew worse, not least when some of the more radical protesters went off to storm the parliament. Police opened fire and killed four protesters.

The government resigned on 28 January 2014 but stayed in place to hold new elections. American officials, including the US Ambassador, Geoffrey R. Pyatt, were busy fixing the results – from the Kremlin perspective. The Americans wanted to 'fuck' the EU and also sideline 'the top dog' in the Maidan, Vitali Klitschko. Nor did they want any Svoboda leaders. The man who was to 'midwife' the coup was Joe Biden, the US Vice President. Critics of the US blame Biden's (still) secret diplomacy behind the coup in 2014 for setting the scene for the future wars in the region. The Russians accused Washington of funding and arming the Maidan protesters and even training some of them in the US Embassy grounds in Kyiv. Certainly, the Americans had been spending large sums of money to back pro-Western groups. One of the main conduits was the US-funded National Endowment for Democracy (NED), set up in 1983.

The Kremlin accused the NED of trying to revive the Cold War. Yet again, the Russians reminded America (and Britain) that they were joint guarantors of Ukrainian security under the terms of the 1994 Budapest Memorandum, under which Kyiv gave up its nuclear weapons. (Ukraine had the third largest stockpile in the world, although the missile codes were controlled by the Russians.) The Kremlin warned that Russia might have to intervene to maintain the agreement.

Meanwhile the fighting around the Maidan camp looked more like real fighting, not protest. On 18 February police opened fire and at least seventeen protesters were killed and many injured. Rioters started looting armouries and police stations around the country but especially in Western Ukraine. Violence between 18–20 February led to a death toll of eighty-five civilians and eighteen police and army officials. Although the protesters blamed the police for many of the killings, it was apparent that Svoboda and other far-right-wing militias fired into the crowds as a heavy-duty provocation. Forensic reports indicated that some of the protesters were shot by hunting rifles rather than police weapons.

On 21 February Yanukovych met with opposition leaders and the foreign ministers of Poland, France and Germany, and arranged a political transition. But the far right rejected the deal and armed militias occupied the parliament, now unprotected by police who had been ordered to withdraw. Yanukovych fled and eventually took refuge in Russia. Putin had invested much time and money in Yanukovich and so the American-backed coup was a big humiliation for Putin. The massive Russian Gazprom company told the new government that it was negotiating the gas supply contract. When the new Kyiv government demurred, the supply to the whole country was cut off in mid-winter. Kyiv had to back down and Putin had made clear who was the Boss.

The start of civil war

The new government, to the Kremlin at least, appeared to be an American puppet as Arseniy Yatsenyuk, who became the prime minister, in turn rewarded the right-wing Svoboda party with three seats in his cabinet. It seemed more like a pro-Western coup than a revolution.

In Crimea, on the night of 26/27 February, Russian special forces seized the Supreme Soviet of the Crimea and the council of ministers' building. They said they were a Crimean militia. Other unmarked troops – the 'little green men' – took over other key installations on the peninsula. The hundred members of the Crimean parliament were said to have voted for a referendum on independence or integration with Russia (though re-integration with Ukraine was not on the ballot). Many of the MPs were not in the chamber and some of those who were said they were threatened to vote, occasionally at gunpoint. By 2 March Russian troops crossed from the leased naval base at Sevastopol, augmented later by troops from mainland Russia. Putin went into his standard denial mode and said he was not planning to occupy the Crimea.

On 16 March, the Crimea held a referendum in which 91 per cent (in a 81 per cent turnout) voted to secede from Ukraine and re-join Russia (this was a more powerful pro-Russian vote than in a similar referendum in 1991, when Ukraine secured its independence). After token resistance in the face of overwhelming odds, the Ukrainian military withdrew from the Crimea as about half its personnel had defected to join the Russian forces.

Even in Ukraine outside the Crimea many citizens were deeply suspicious of the new Kyiv government. This was not reflected in much of the Western reporting which portrayed the 2014 events as a democratic revolution against a corrupt government.

Opposition was strongest in the Donbas region. In April anti-Kyiv protesters announced the Donetsk People's Republic (DPR) and also said a referendum on the new pro-Russian republic would be held. The Luhansk People's Republic (LPR) followed suit. Both passed the referenda with huge majorities in a very high turnout. The Kremlin certainly supported the moves but urged a delay so the referenda could be independently assessed to avoid the accusation that the polls were rigged – which the West and Kyiv of course claimed anyway.

An attempt to set up an Odessa republic met with much more violence as both pro-Kyiv and anti-Kyiv fought street battles on 2 May. Right-wing militias, especially the Right Sector, entered the fray and forty-eight people were killed. The so-called Odesa massacre further divided the country and no doubt prompted the big result for independence from Ukraine in the Donbas referenda.

In the post-coup presidential elections of 25 May 2014, Petro Poroshenko was elected with a 55 per cent majority, a rare outright victory for the fifth president of Ukraine. The extreme right-wing candidates did very badly. Poroshenko was a hard-line nationalist himself: his campaign motto was military, language and faith. A firm advocate of the Ukrainian language, he was also a supporter of the Ukrainian Orthodox Church's separation from the Moscow Patriarch. The new president had been a foreign minister and had developed strong pro-EU and NATO tendencies. In Ukraine he was most famous for being the 'Chocolate King', as the owner of the Roshen confectionary empire. He was a billionaire and accused of corruption, though new laws had probably caused a decline of business malpractice during his presidency, even though he was cited in the famous Panama and Paradise papers. Like Putin, he was a keen follower of and participant in judo and sambo.

But the most important task facing Poroshenko was ending the growing civil war in the Donbas. Initially, he likened the armed militias there to 'Somali pirates' but soon Kyiv had to start taking them far more seriously. Ukrainian military defectors as well as volunteers, and regulars, from Russia joined the forces of the DPR and LPR. In response the Kyiv government formed new National Guard units. Some of the right-wing militias which had fought in the Maidan joined. One off-shoot of the Right Sector was the Azov Battalion, later Regiment. Although backed by some money from Ukrainian Jewish sources, it was considered by the Kremlin to be a Neo-Nazi organisation, that sported insignia similar to that of the SS. Certainly the Kremlin saw the regiment as a key part of its de-Nazification propaganda. The unit later played a major role in Mariupol, its main base, during the next ten years of fighting.

Summary of situation in 2014

The Kremlin had begun to retreat into a 'Fortress Russia' mentality as domestic critics were traduced as 'national traitors' and 'fifth columnists'. Putin was possibly correct in arguing that the collapse of the USSR had been a tragedy for his version of his country. But he was wrong in entirely blaming the West; the main causes of the implosion of the USSR were domestic. Nationalism was just one of the centrifugal forces in the creaking government structures, along with the failure of economic reform, though geopolitical competition between the West and the USSR successor states could not be ignored. And Ukraine was a central element of the crisis of post-Soviet Eurasia.

The change of government in Kyiv in February 2014 transformed the demographic balance of power: from the south and east to the west. Yanukovych's government was replaced by one in which around 60 per cent of the top leadership came from the four former Habsburg provinces (about 12 per cent of the population). Previously 75 per cent of the leadership came from the south and east, with 42 per cent from Donetsk (Yanukovych's home province). The south and east accounted for 50 per cent of the total population.

This shift in influence fired up Putin's fear that the West was pushing Russia out of the whole of Ukraine. The Kremlin's decision to invade Crimea was primarily, but not solely, intended to protect a very specific asset in Ukraine: the naval base for the Black Sea Fleet. This was as much desperation as aggression. Putin had tried more financial assistance to the Yanukovych government and then economic pressures and also diplomacy with the West. The 2014 annexation emboldened the pro-Russian politicians in the Crimea as well as separatist tendencies in the majority of the peninsula's population while it hardened the attitudes of the government in Kyiv. This led to what the London International Institute of Strategic Studies called a 'deeply flawed plebiscite'. Under the watchful eyes of regular Russian troops in unmarked uniforms 97 per cent allegedly supported the return to Russia.[4]

President Barack Obama announced that the USA and the international community would never recognize the referendum. The US also offered loans and more security assistance to the new prime minister in Kyiv, Arseniy Yatsenyuk, a lawyer and economist, who was to serve twice in the role; he also became the first Ukrainian prime minister to visit the White House. Sanctions were imposed on the Kremlin, both military and economic, while the US sent more aircraft and warships to assist

NATO members closest to Russia. As the NATO Deputy Secretary General, Alexander Vershbow, put it: 'For twenty years the security of the Euro-Atlantic region has been based on the premise that we do not face an adversary to our east. This premise is now in doubt.'

A war of words reminiscent of the First Cold War erupted. Speaking to a St Petersburg press conference on 24 May 2014, Putin put his case clearly:

> Some of the recent events in Ukraine directly threaten our interests, first of all with regard to security. I'm talking about Ukraine's potential accession to NATO. ... Such an accession could be followed by the deployment of missile strike systems in Ukraine, including Crimea. Should this happen, it would have serious geopolitical consequences for our country. In fact Russia would be forced out of the Black Sea territory, a region for legitimate presence, in which Russia has fought for centuries. ... Our Western partners encouraged an unconstitutional regime change. This is exactly what I call resolving disputes using force. And we have responded to this force. Why? ... Because the interests of the Russian nation and the Russian state were at stake. Those who started this should have thought of that.

To support his views, Putin ordered the state-controlled media to portray the Kyiv government as a fascist junta which was intent on carrying out extreme punitive measures against its own citizens, especially native Russian speakers. Washington was pulling all the strings. And the Kremlin was simply helping the Crimean people and those in the two new republics to stop Kyiv's murder and brutality. In 2014 Putin's domestic rating soared to 88 per cent; few Western leaders' popularity could compare. Despite the frequent poll rigging, Putin's popularity was largely genuine then. So the opponents of Putin had to choose between emigration or remaining in silence. Critics risked political suicide and prison, otherwise. The bravest critic was Alexie Navalny of mixed Ukrainian and Russian stock. He was a lawyer and an anti-corruption activist, who was very adept at using social media. He described Russia's ruling party, United Russia, as a 'party of crooks and thieves', which became a popular war cry. Navalny was poisoned with the Kremlin favourite, Novichok, and imprisoned again after bravely, or foolishly, returning from life-saving treatment in Germany.

Peace Accords

After months of heavy fighting in the Donbas in 2014, peace talks were held in the capital of Belarus, Minsk. France and Germany and the fifty-seven-member Organization of Security and Cooperation in Europe held the ring while the Kremlin and Kyiv signed the Minsk Protocol on 5 September. This deal did not end the conflict but the more active inclusion of the DPR and LPR led, in February 2015, to the Minsk 2 agreement that did reduce tension. This ceasefire held and a thirty-kilometre-wide buffer zone was established, and prisoners were released by both sides. Over 700 OSCE ceasefire observers remained in place until 2022. Casualties dropped dramatically.

The vast majority of casualties in the civil war occurred in the first period before Minsk 2 started to kick in. Perhaps as many as 14,400 people were killed between 2014 and 2021. Approximately 3,000 were civilians, while up to 4,500 pro-government combatants were killed; separatist force fatalities numbered over 6,000. There were many faults with the Minsk accords but to some extent they eventually worked – for a while. They were often criticized for being too complicated and both sides accused each other of bad faith. The Kremlin argued that this was a civil war in which they were not involved except for some humanitarian measures. But the American Department of Defense said in March 2016 that the Kremlin maintained 'command and control' over the DPR and LPR republics and that 'Russia was pouring heavy weapons into the Donbas'.

Fundamentally even a flawed ceasefire was better than all-out war – or so most of the Minsk negotiators seemed to believe. Would the separatist republics in Ukraine become another frozen post-Soviet crisis zone, along with Transnistria, South Ossetia, Abkhazia and Nagorno-Karabakh or would the civil war fester into all-out war?

Chapter Three

A Man Called Volodymyr

Volodymyr Zelensky was born, on 25 January 1978, into a Ukrainian Jewish family in Kryvyi Rih, then in the Ukrainian Soviet Socialist Republic of the USSR. Russian was his first language, though today he speaks fluent Ukrainian and good English. The family spent four years in the Mongolian city of Erdenet, a copper-mining centre where up to half of the workers were also Russians.

The young Volodymyr went to elementary school back in Ukraine and was later offered a scholarship to study in Israel at 16, but his father stopped him going. Later he earned a law degree at the Kryvyi Rih Institute of Economics but the young man never practised as a lawyer; what attracted him was entertainment, not law. At 17 he had started taking part in KVN comedy competitions. This was a Russian comedy television show and international competition in which teams, usually composed of college students, competed with comedy sketches. Zelensky helped found the comedy outfit, called Kvartal 95 that performed mainly in Moscow but also in Ukraine and in post-Soviet countries.

Kvartal 95 started producing for Ukrainian TV in 2003 and then moved into feature films – rom-coms. In 2008 Zelensky starred in the romantic lead role of a highly sexed very clean-shaven dentist called Igor. The film, set in New York, was called *Love in the Big City* – it was a hit in Russia (though the sequel was banned in Ukraine). Zelensky, whom some accused of having a small-man complex, also starred as *Napoleon* in 2012 that was itself a sequel to the rather bizarre comedy set in the final days of the Reich called *Hitler Goes Kaput* (which did not include the future president). Zelensky was perhaps better known for voicing the Ukrainian dubbing of the little bear in *Paddington* and *Paddington 2* – perhaps an irony for the man who became most famous for standing up to the very big bear.

At the height of his film career, Zelensky was very vocal in his criticism of the intention of the Ukrainian Ministry of Culture to ban Russian artists and films (that's why Zelensky's Russian-language sequel to *Love in the Big City* was banned in 2018). When the 2022 war began, Russian artists wanted Zelensky's films in Russian banned, especially after it was reported that Kvartal 95 had made big donations to the Ukrainian army. Zelensky's best-known acting role, however, was as the accidental president of Ukraine in the 2015 TV series *Servant of the People*. Zelensky played a high-school teacher, Vasily Petrovych Goloborodko (Vasil Holorodko), who won the election after a video of his ranting against government corruption went viral. Another TV series (*Svaty*, about in-laws) was banned in Ukraine in 2017 but unbanned when he became president. Zelensky usually made feature films in his first language, Russian, but he did make a Ukrainian-language romantic-comedy in 2018.

Life imitates art

Zelensky was later to campaign against cronyism but he made a close work colleague, Ivan Bakanov, head of the SBU, the Ukrainian Security Service. In October 2021 the International Consortium of Investigative Journalists published what became known as the 'Pandora Papers'. *Inter alia*, they revealed that both senior Ukrainians leaders had offshore companies in the British Virgin Islands, Belize and Cyprus. These companies also owned upmarket London properties. When Zelensky became president he did hand over his shares in major offshore companies to another old colleague but money appears to have been still paid to the Zelensky family. Although Zelensky in both roles – TV and actual president – had sworn to clean up government, the imminent war with Russia took precedence in public opinion. Some senior politicians (not ex-comedians) actually joked that nearly every Ukrainian had offshore companies, including small market-stall holders.

Zelensky's TV persona as president became so popular that he was regularly shown to be leading in opinion polls months before he had been registered for the April 2019 election. His fictitious party was registered as an official party to avoid other politicians usurping the wildly popular Servant of the People brand. On New Year's Eve in 2019 Zelensky finally admitted he was standing as a candidate which upstaged the New Year's address of the incumbent president, Petro Poroshenko, a former businessman and politician who served as the fifth president of Ukraine from 2014 to 2019.

Zelensky's campaign was largely virtual; he deployed social media and YouTube clips. He also did stand-up routines portraying himself as anti-establishment and anti-corruption. But his critics accused him of being in hock to Ihor Kolomoyskyi, a Ukrainian-born Israeli-Cypriot billionaire and media mogul who owned the company that broadcast the *Servant of the People* TV series. Kolomoyskyi was one of the richest oligarchs and a pillar of the Jewish community but he was accused of numerous shady deals. The Americans banned him from the USA and Zelensky, very sensitive to accusations of cronyism and corruption, distanced himself from the banking and media magnate.

During the election some critics said that voting for a comic actor would benefit only Russia, though few mentioned how successful the former actor Ronald Reagan had been in standing up to what he called the 'Evil Empire'.

Zelensky easily won the first round of elections, and also the second round on 21 April 2019 when he secured 73 per cent of the vote to Poroshenko's 25 per cent. The leaders of the European Union rushed to congratulate Zelensky, especially the French president, Emmanuel Macron.

Zelensky was inaugurated as the first Jewish president of Ukraine; Vlodymyr Groysman was made the (second) Jewish prime minster. Except for Israel, this was first country to have a Jewish head of state *and* head of government. This religious point is made because a Jewish leadership does make it harder to swallow the Kremlin line that the

Ukrainian government was neo-Nazi or Nazi (although there is no doubt that Ukrainian neo-Nazi militia units were active).

Zelensky soon found out that it was easier to poke fun at politicians than to be a successful one himself. He failed to get some of his promised reforms through the parliament *(Rada)* but he did get a law passed ending the legal immunity of lawmakers. This was one of his key campaign pledges. Zelensky was also criticized for taking power away from some of the oligarchs, including media moguls but then used some of this influence to aggregate his own power base instead. The newly installed president, a political novice, did make some questionable appointments – not least elevating former colleagues in Kvartal 95. Most egregiously, Ivan Bakanov became head of the Ukrainian Secret Service. He was even made a lieutenant, the minimum military rank to allow him to access secret papers. Bakanov was a childhood friend of the president and he had already been made head of the Servant of the People party; he kept the security portfolio from 2019 to 2022 when the top spy was sacked by his oldest friend, Zelensky.

Nevertheless, Zelensky remained wildly popular. In July 2019, his party had won the first ever single-party majority in the parliament with the Servant of the People party winning 254 out of 424 seats. Zelensky was criticized for bringing in novices. One opponent said he had allowed in some dubious MPs: 'the unemployed, wedding photographers, showmen, restaurateurs, most with very average educational backgrounds and limited knowledge'. Yet at the same time he was attacked for deploying some of the old guard, notably Arsen Avakov, who were kept on as ministers despite allegations of corruption. The argument was that such a novice administration needed some old hands. Zelensky was the first to admit that he was an apprentice and, specifically, not an economics expert. Zelensky's popularity began to wane especially as he failed to live up to his electoral pledges to resolve the 2014 occupation of the Crimea and the simmering war in the Donbas.

Zelensky appointed Leonid Kuchma, a former president, as the Ukrainian representative on the so-called Tripartite Contact Group that was trying to reach a settlement. In July 2019 Zelensky spoke to Putin for the first time on the phone and they discussed the European mediation efforts as well as prisoner exchanges. In October 2019, Zelensky struck a provisional deal with the separatists in the Donbas in which the Ukrainian government would respect elections in the 'liberated areas' if the Russians troops, none in formal Russian uniforms, returned to the motherland.

Zelensky came under heavy fire from his own side. Most of the pro-Ukrainians in the occupied areas had been driven out so there would almost inevitably be a pro-Moscow majority, even if (a big if) the elections were free and fair. And would the Russians keep their word and withdraw their forces? Moreover, many right-wing Ukrainian militias, including the far-right Azov force, said they would not accept this agreement even if it actually worked. The fighting continued in the Donbas.

The French and Germans, however, resumed their mediation efforts that had been dubbed the Normandy Format, which had been abandoned in 2016. It was so named because the French, Germans, Russians and Ukrainians first met informally in 2014 during the seventieth anniversary of D Day commemorations in Normandy, France. This renewal in December 2019 was the occasion for the first meeting between the two warring presidents. In July 2020 Zelensky announced a formal ceasefire with the separatists – the twentieth since 2014. The fighting continued but ceasefire violations were reduced.

Zelensky was also anxious to court another president, Joe Biden. Zelensky's infamous phone call with President Donald Trump had been embroiled in a major scandal which was a catalyst for an impeachment enquiry against 'the Donald'. Its essence was that Trump would withhold an aid package to Ukraine of $400 million if Zelensky refused to dish the (alleged) dirt on Joe Biden and his son Hunter's alleged involvement with a Ukrainian natural gas company. The Ukrainian president denied that he had been pressurized by Trump but, under the circumstances, what else could Zelensky say?

In September 2021 Zelensky paid a state visit to Biden and also met the top defence officials including Lloyd Austin, the Secretary of Defense. Just after Zelensky gave a speech to the United Nations his closest aide, Serhiy Shefir, was attacked in his car in Ukraine. Shefir escaped injury but his driver was hit by three bullets, although he recovered. And so coup rumours proliferated in Kyiv. After the US visit, Zelensky continued to press for NATO membership, the ultimate red rag for the Kremlin. Though the Russian military build-up on the Ukrainian borders made Kyiv's desire to be embraced by the EU and NATO even more pressing, it was once again the action-reaction cycle that characterized the First Cold War.

And yet it was ironic that as the drumbeats of war intensified, Zelensky called on the West not to create 'a panic' about an imminent invasion threat as this was undermining the Ukrainian economy. The Ukrainian president seemed to disagree publicly with Biden's assessment that an invasion was imminent. On 19 February 2022, at the annual Munich Security Conference, Zelensky gave a powerful speech even though the CIA had warned him that the Russians might try to stage a coup in Kyiv while he was – briefly – away. It was again deeply ironic that Zelensky should now call for 'an end of appeasement' in Munich of all places. He referred to the 1994 Budapest Protocols when he said: 'Ukraine has been granted security assurances in exchange for giving up the world's third-largest nuclear arsenal. We don't have any firearms and there's no security.'

A few hours before the invasion, Zelensky recorded an address to both Ukraine and Russia explaining that he had no intention of attacking the Donbas and then he spoke in Russian telling the Russian people to prevent war, even though he knew that the Kremlin would not broadcast his appeal for peace.

War leader

The Russian invasion would turn the former comic into a famous war leader. Zelensky's popularity in the West would soon rival the 'Gorbymania' of the 1980s. Perhaps it required the tribulations of war to show what was really hidden behind the greasepaint. And behind every great man there is usually an even greater female. Olena Kiyashko married Zelensky in 2003; they had known each at school and university and they worked together in Kvartal 95. She had grave doubts about his becoming president and yet she became a key architect of his political career. She also forged an international image as first lady, for example the first foreign first lady to address the US Congress.

When offered exile by the USA as Russia invaded, Zelensky is reputed to have said 'I need ammunition not a ride', though his biographer questioned this.[1] Likewise, First Lady Olena stood by her man in Kyiv, despite American offers of a refuge and despite at least ten assassination attempts, perhaps not all on the order of the Kremlin.

According to Olena, her husband is 'very honest and a workaholic'. And she says he cannot relax. 'He gives the impression that he is a jolly guy and a joker but when we go on vacations, it is not until the third day that he cuts loose and safely looks around.'[2]

The real question of Zelensky's leadership is whether he could be a better actor than his deadly rival, Putin. The Russian leader had played many roles, especially with Western politicians. He had pretended that the Russian troops were not in Georgia, Transnistria and Syria and then, after 2014, in Ukraine. Both men's fates depended on the war and on their stamina, wiliness, agility, courage and sheer determination to survive, let alone win. Acting would not be enough.

Chapter Four

A Man Called Vladimir

Background

Vladimir Putin was born in Leningrad (later renamed Saint Petersburg) in October 1952. And he grew up in Baskov Lane; despite the name, it was a straight wide street that had once boasted elegant nineteenth-century apartments that had become shabby and dilapidated. He was a cherished only surviving child as his two brothers died young; one, Viktor, died partly because of starvation caused by the long Wehrmacht siege of the city. Vladimir's mother, Maria, was a factory worker and his father, Vladimir, had been conscripted as a submariner in the navy but later served in a 'destruction battalion' of the internal security police, the NKVD. These units were notoriously ruthless in conducting scorched-earth tactics as the Germans advanced rapidly in the early stages of Operation BARBAROSSA and they hunted down pro-German partisans and anti-Russian units in the Baltic States. Vladimir senior later served in the regular army where he was badly wounded.

The Putin family had solid party and military backgrounds; a number of relatives were also killed by the Germans in the Great Patriotic War. To add to the ideological credentials, Spiridon Putin, President Vladimir's grandfather, was a personal cook for Lenin and Stalin. In another historical rhyme, the role of a personal chef was to play a key role in the president's later career.

At primary school young Vladimir did not join the Young Pioneers, though he did take up judo and sambo, a martial art popular in the USSR. He was a smallish boy but was considered very tough because he would keep on fighting even when initially overwhelmed by bigger boys. He later studied German in which he became proficient, especially during his KGB career. Putin went on to study law at the Leningrad State University; while there he had to join the communist party not least in order to be awarded his first degree. (Much later, in 1997, he received the equivalent of a PhD with a thesis on the strategic planning of the mining economy. High-flyers in mid-career were expected to demonstrate heavyweight intellectual potential by publishing a book or completing a doctorate. Some Western academics have alleged that part of the thesis was plagiarized.)

In 1975 Putin joined the KGB in Leningrad. After his training, he worked in the 'Second Chief Directorate' in counter-intelligence before he was transferred to the First Chief Directorate. There he monitored foreigners, especially consular staff in Leningrad. His progress was slow but in 1984 he was sent to Moscow for further training. From 1985 to 1990 he was based in Dresden in the East German Republic, where his cover was as a translator. Although officially he played a junior role in wireless communications, he was alleged to have been involved with handling and arming members of the Red Army Faction that committed many acts of terrorism in West Germany. When the Wall fell, Putin was kept busy destroying some of the key secret files while spiriting some away to Moscow.

Putin's role in Dresden was by definition shadowy. Away from the prying eyes of a small army of Western counter-intelligence agents in East and West Berlin, it was an important centre for financial smuggling for the KGB; and some of the money may have been used to fund the role of the KGB *after* the fall of the Wall both in the West and in a new Russia. Putin could have been central in rebuilding the power of the KGB in the Russian Federation.[1]

After Dresden, whether he resigned his role in the active KGB service or whether he was pushed is unclear. With the rank of lieutenant colonel, Putin worked for a few months with the international affairs section of the Leningrad State University, while beginning his doctoral research.

Within a year Putin was working in the office of Leningrad's mayor, Anatoly Sobchak, as head of foreign relations and, especially, international investment. Despite anti-corruption allegations aimed at him, he remained in post until 1996. At the same time, he was active in local politics, organising the Saint Petersburg branch of the Our Home party that was founded by Viktor Chernomyrdin; this was a pro-business centrist party that backed Boris Yeltsin. In June 1996 Putin lost some of his patronage when Mayor Sobchak was not re-elected, and moved to Moscow where he was in charge of the property owned by the state abroad and managed the transfer of former assets of the USSR and their removal to the new Russian Federation.

After (apparently) slow progress in the KGB and senior civil service work in a relative backwater in Saint Petersburg, Putin was thrust centre stage and considered a rapidly rising star, especially by his mentor, the affable but drunken President Yeltsin. In March 1997 Yeltsin made Putin his deputy chief of the presidential staff. Yeltsin kept promoting his protégé and in July 1998 he became head of the Federal Security Service (FSB), the direct successor to the KGB; there he could buttress the metamorphosis of the KGB into the FSB. In August 1999 Yeltsin made Putin the acting prime minister (the fifth in less than eighteen months) and announced that he wanted him to be his successor. And yet Putin was almost unknown; many seasoned politicians thought he would go the way of other recent Yeltsin appointees.

Putin had many better-known rivals. But he had advantages that the others didn't. Besides the ailing President Yeltsin's support, he had law and order and security credentials. He had taken a very hard-line approach to the Second Chechen War as well as the invasion of Dagestan by Jihadists. One of the tipping points was the bombing of four apartment blocks in September 1999 in the Russian cities of Buynaksk, Moscow and Volgodonsk, killing more than 300 and injuring more than 1,000, and spreading a wave of fear and panic across the country. The attacks were blamed on Chechen Islamists and this resulted in the full-scale second war in Chechnya. It also massively boosted support for the former KGB colonel. While he was not formally a member of a party, Putin said he backed the Unity Party that won the second largest percentage of the popular vote in the Duma elections of December 1999.

The perpetrators of the apartment attacks were said to be Chechens but many Western critics, both in intelligence and academia, have insisted it was a false-flag operation by the FSB.

On 31 December 1999 Yeltsin resigned without any fanfare and, constitutionally, Putin became acting president of the Russian Federation. On the same day that he took office Putin signed a decree that the outgoing president and his relatives would not be faced with any corruption charges. This later applied to Putin who had been involved with dodgy deals in Saint Peterburg. One of the main charges related to massive kickbacks by the Swiss-based Mabetex company that specialized in major construction contracts, in Russia's case projects to renovate the Duma, the main Opera House and even the Kremlin.

In the presidential election of March 2000, Putin won in the first round with 53 per cent of the vote. Vladimir had now finally arrived as the top dog but he faced a massive challenge to stabilize the Russian Federation after the collapse of the USSR. To his credit this is what Putin largely did and he achieved genuine popularity.

If he had retired after the constitutionally allowed two terms of the presidency his legacy would have been secure. Yet like all autocratic leaders he did not know when to call time.

The nuclear-powered submarine *Kursk* sank in an accident on 12 August 2000 in the Barents Sea, during the first major Russian naval exercise in more than ten years, and all 118 submariners died. Bearing in mind Putin's own father's role as a submariner, and the president's determination to rebuild the crumbling defence forces, it was odd that it took several days for the president to break off from his vacation and several more days before he visited the location of the sinking.

In October 2002, Moscow's Dubrovka theatre was engulfed in a massive hostage crisis. Chechen rebels were eventually overcome by Russian special forces but up to 170 victims died, including many innocents who were gassed, fatally, by the special-force would-be rescuers.

Despite these two crises, Putin's tough-guy image and stabilization of the economy led to a continued rise in his popularity. The Second War in Chechnya was brought to a sort of end by brutal Russian army methods and a switch of sides by key Chechen leaders. The independence movement was hobbled but occasional attacks were still mounted in the northern Caucasus and in the Russian Federation. An example of another alleged Chechen conspiracy was the Beslan school siege in North Ossetia in September 2004 when over 333 were killed, mainly children, during a botched security-force intervention.

Putin was more successful in playing the hard man in his relations with the oligarchs. In what was called the 'grand bargain', via force and bribery, the Kremlin persuaded most of the super-rich oligarchs to either join Putin or just stay out of politics completely. Those who openly opposed Putin would soon see the inside of the country's grimmest prisons or be outside in comfortable but nervous exile, forever fearing the knock on the door even in Paris or London.

The continuing terror attacks encouraged Putin to prioritise internal security while his crackdown on the oligarchs added to his popularity as well as his personal power. In the second presidential election. Putin won 71 per cent of the vote. Putin tried to restore some of the cradle-to-grave benefits of the old Soviet Union, the dissolution of which he described as the 'greatest geopolitical catastrophe of the twentieth century'. In 2005 Putin launched the so-called national priority projects to improve education, housing and healthcare.

Initially, Putin allowed some free media and opposition criticism but two people were singled out to stress the limits of criticism. Mikhail Khodorkovsky was the richest man in Russia, the head of Yukos Oil and Gas company. The business magnate wanted a more open society in Russia and so fell foul of Putin. Khodorkovsky was jailed for fraud and tax evasion and spent over ten years in prison, and then sought exile in Switzerland and, finally, the UK.

Another Putin opponent silenced was Anna Politkovskaya who was born in New York of Ukrainian Soviet diplomat parents. She became famous for exposing the corruption and atrocities of the Russian army in the Chechen wars. She wrote for the prominent independent *Novaya Gazeta*; nevertheless, Politkovskaya was threatened with rape, faced mock executions, and almost died from a Putin-era speciality: poisoning.

Eventually, she was murdered on 7 October 2006 in the elevator of her Moscow apartment – her martyrdom spelled the beginning of the end of any free media in Russia. She wrote in the UK *Guardian* that

> We are hurtling back into a Soviet abyss, into an information vacuum that spells death from our own ignorance. All we have left is the internet, where information is still freely available. For the rest, if you want to go on working as a journalist, it's total servility to Putin. Otherwise, it can be death, the bullet, poison, or trial – whatever our special services, Putin's guard dogs, see fit.[2]

Shortly after the journalist's murder, Putin showed another side of his bullying manner. In January 2007 he entertained Angela Merkel, the German Chancellor, at his Black Sea residence. Although the political background – blackmail regarding Russian gas and oil supplies – was more significant it was the presence of Putin's large black female Labrador retriever, Konni, that caused the most media attention. Merkel was a well-known dog-phobic and Putin knew that. When Konni planted herself next to Merkel, the unnerved chancellor gave what was termed a 'classic Merkel eye-roll'.

Merkel later confided, 'I understand why he has to do this – to prove he's a man. He's afraid of his own weaknesses. Russia has nothing, no successful politics or economy.'

She did not mention that Russia *did* have lots of oil and gas.

A major weakness inherited by Putin was the expansion of NATO. The Kremlin boss, like many senior Russians, had always believed that Germany was allowed to be unified on the condition that NATO did not expand any further. That was seen as the Western price for unification and was a genuine belief in the Russian hierarchy. In the February 2007 Munich Security Conference, Putin formally complained about the expansion of US power and warned that NATO should expand no further eastwards. Soon previous arms control arrangements began to deteriorate, not least when Russia moved openly into Transnistria and parts of Georgia. The tough-guy stance continued to generate some domestic support, however. In the December 2007 parliamentary elections, the United Russia party that backed Putin had won almost 65 per cent of the popular vote.

Castling

In chess when a rook and a king swap places, in order to shore up the defence, it is called castling (*rokirovka*). Putin was barred from holding a third successive term as president so the First Deputy Prime Minister, Dmitry Medvedev, was chosen as Putin's successor. A day later, on 8 May 2008, Putin became prime minster. Nobody was fooled: he was still in charge.

By 2011 large protests throughout Russia complained of electoral fraud and the FSB started to fret about a 'colour revolution' as had happened in a number of neighbouring countries. Behind the scenes militia groups were organized, loyal to the United Russia party and to Putin personally. Meanwhile, Medvedev made it clear that there would be another castling. In March 2012, Putin won the presidential election with over 63 per cent of the vote. Internationally, and in Russia, the media proclaimed fraud while inside the federation numerous pro- and anti-Putin protests kept boiling.

Although social reforms were again promised in Putin's newest presidency, the laws against homosexuality secured headlines, especially in the West. Putin also started to promote the All-Russia People's Front, that he headed. It was designed as a mass movement as the pro-Putin United Russia party had begun to lose support.

Rebuilding the military

Putin wanted to restore Russian greatness after the humiliation of the immediate post-Soviet period. The new leader inherited a military relic. The manning system was not entirely dissimilar from the pre-Soviet feudal model, based on conscription and mass mobilization for war to top up the large standing army that had no professional cadre below warrant officers. Hazing was ubiquitous and vicious and the relationship between officers and conscripts was redolent of master-serf relationships. The command and control was rigid and antiquated. Above all, corruption was endemic especially regarding weapons procurement.

Under Defence Minister Anatoly Serdyukov major reforms had been introduced in 2009. The aim was to reduce the bloated size and make the armed forces more professional, as nearly all the NATO forces had given up conscription. There was a need for flexible, highly mobile professional expeditionary forces, a sharp contrast to the lumbering stolidity of the old Red Army.

The chain of command was also improved. Officer numbers (except for lieutenants) were reduced – the number of chiefs versus Indians was ridiculous, almost as bad as the UK Royal Navy which, until recently, boasted more admirals than capital ships. The plan was to reduce the Russian armed forces to below one million (while in Britain the army was reduced to under 80,000) and creating professional NCO corps. Drastic changes were made in training as well. At the break-up of the USSR 397 civilian institutions of higher education had military departments. This was reduced eventually to ninety-three military centres in civilian institutions.

The downsizing was supposed to have been accomplished by around 2020. Just over 220,000 officers, 425,00 contract servicemen and women and 300,000 annual conscripts were planned.

The military districts were re-organized as well into seven areas; the naval commands were similarly re-jigged. Some of the many defence buildings, especially in Moscow, were scheduled to be sold off, not least to improve housing for troops. The Russians, despite the reductions, did not seem to be wallowing in post-cold war dividends. Before the reforms, it was often estimated that only 13–15 per cent of army units were combat-ready.

The air force was modernized and rationalized as well. The number of air bases was reduced from 245 to 52. Likewise, the unwieldy Soviet model for the navy was rationalized and modernized, including the building of modern nuclear hunter-killer submarines. Naval aviation and naval infantry (marines) were revamped. Despite all the debate in Russian military circles about airborne troops, only four independent airborne/air assault brigades were created. The personnel in the Strategic Missile and Space Forces were slightly reduced and re-organized as well.

And yet much of the structure of the armed forces worked against modernization and especially individual initiative in combat. A once revolutionary army had long become sclerotic.[3] Russia had over 25,000 military bases and garrisons that were effectively closed towns under military rule. Local councils did not want to take them over and they sometimes became not only run-down but lawless. Likewise, the General Staff resisted most of the reforms for almost a decade into Putin's imperium. The Kremlin leader had very little military background – just a few months' training during his intelligence induction. Despite the lip service, the military top brass were sometimes reluctant to follow his lead; and this persisted even into the Ukraine wars.

Budgets were increased; the official figures put the number at 3.2 per cent of GDP (2013) to 3.7 per cent from 2015. This was a rise of around 60 per cent to 3 trillion roubles ($583 billion). Whether any of these figures could be trusted is another matter.

Despite the much-vaunted reforms and super weapons, such as the Armata tanks and hypersonic missiles, Russian military might was still often a hollowed-out Potemkin makeshift, largely because of continuing endemic corruption. Money was allocated to improve equipment and the conditions for ordinary soldiers – from useless cardboard body armour and helmets to boots that fell rapidly apart. A classic example was the *Ekaterinburg* SSNN Delta-class submarine commissioned in the last period of the USSR. It caught fire through shoddy servicing while in dry dock in late December 2011. Another series of minor fires ensued. It was initially stated that all the weapons had been removed. They had not been. The funds allocated to pay for the expensive removal of the nuclear ballistic missiles had disappeared and so the weapons had remained. The fires could have spread to the nukes, conventional missiles and the torpedoes. It took some years before the sub was ready for service. Likewise, numerous ammunition depots were spread around the country.

Some of the equipment and ammunition went back as far as the Second World War and even the 1920s. Rusty old tanks miraculously emerged as the Russians searched around for replacement equipment in late 2022 after the massive losses of armour in Ukraine.

'Final term'?

Putin's fourth term of office began on May 2018 after winning another presidential election with over 76 per cent of the vote. It became clear, however, that Putin would again work around the constitutional limitations for president by initiating constitutional amendments to extend his presidential powers by two six-year terms starting in 2020. He continued to supply bread and circuses for the masses, not least by hosting the Soche Winter Olympics in 2014 and the FIFA World Cup in October 2018. The Russian population might tolerate censorship and political oppression but the economic chaos of the Yeltsin period had shown that economic stability was the determinant of political survival. Putin did attempt economic reforms in the beginning and then moved towards a form of state capitalism by controlling or exiling and jailing some oligarchs. Then came the world financial crisis of 2008. The current period from 2014 and especially 2022 brought war and sanctions.

But Putin could not have fully prepared for Covid. He somewhat undermined his own macho image by his largely absentee leadership during the pandemic. He self-isolated to an extreme level, symbolized by pictures of his sitting at one end of a massive table when he was filmed consulting with his increasingly distant, and apparently increasingly hawkish, small coterie of close advisers.

Putin's ideas

In the history of Russian dictators, leaders are supposed to be published intellectuals as well as political experts. In July 2021 Putin published a famous essay, quoted by many and carefully read by a few, called *On the Historical Unity of Russians and Ukrainians*.[4] Putin in essence said that

Ukraine did not exist as an independent sovereign state and he warned that Ukraine's accession to NATO would be a 'red-line issue' for Russia. The Kremlin repeatedly denied that Russia was about to invade the country even though very large troop build-ups around Ukraine's border indicated the contrary. On 21 February 2022 the Kremlin formally recognized the two separatist republics in the Donbas.

On 24 February 2022 the tectonic plates of world politics shifted when Russa invaded its sovereign neighbour. Putin called it a 'special military operation' and punished or threatened to punish any Russians who dared to call it what it was: a full-scale invasion. He claimed he was protecting the predominantly Russian speakers in the Donbas from genocide at worst and humiliation at best. He insisted the country was run by Nazis, despite the Jewish president.

Putin may be a cynical Machiavellian operator but he also is a sincere believer in restoring Russia as a great power. To do this, he has elevated ex-KGB cronies who are determined to control the state and then use Russian secret service techniques abroad, not least in using big financial laundromats such as London. In setting up various domestic think tanks and encouraging some conservative scholars, Putin has tried to introduce a cultural and political revolution both at home and abroad. He has attacked globalism and neo-liberalism and has lined up with China to lead a new anti-American system. In this he has earned much support, not just from fellow autocrats in Iran but also in much of the anti-colonial global south, much of it lauded by the newly expanded BRICS group. At the height of the Ukraine war, for example, a major Commonwealth country such as South Africa conducted major naval exercises with Russia and China.

Although Russia's fundamental problem is that it has not de-colonized itself, the Kremlin rhetoric does strike many welcome chords with much of Africa, Asia and South America.

The restoration of Russian greatness abroad and at home is allied with a number of conservative agendas, for example a close collaboration with the Russian Orthodox Church. In 2012 the head of the Church in Moscow, Patriarch Kirill (Cyril), likened Putin to 'a miracle of God';

presumably a fan of the president then. Putin does attend the Church on the main holy days and appears to be a believer despite his nostalgia for the avowedly atheistic USSR. But, like Stalin's use of religion in the Great Patriotic War, Putin can clearly see the advantages of getting God on his side in the war with the West.

Although Putin has fallen out with prominent Jewish oligarchs, by and large the Russian Jewish community see him as a force for stability. Despite the attacks on the Jewish president of Ukraine, the World Jewish Congress did praise Putin for making Russia 'a country where Jews are welcome'.

Despite his attacks on Western sexual immorality, Putin has also co-operated with and even promoted people he knew to be gay. What he doesn't like is political opponents who will undermine his crusade to save Russia from Western values, including trans issues, and threaten to undermine Russian culture and traditions.

Fighting back

Putin has tried, above all, to shore up Russian prestige and power. This has centred on the prevention of NATO expansion although his full-throttled attack on Ukraine did the exact opposite. The Kremlin's focus has been on the south as much as the West, however. Ukraine had to be brought back into the Kremlin orbit, in Putin's reasoning. Syria was an important location of military bases and a port in the Mediterranean and a major ally in the Middle East. In the east, China was a key ally but so was India, the largest customer for Russian military equipment (though the fall-out from Ukraine is likely to wipe out Russian arms sales in the future, except to the most desperate of allies). Putin has also worked hard to co-operate with the post-Soviet states in central Asia.

Relations with the USA improved under Trump but have reached a new very low point with Joe Biden, not least with the Democratic president's passionate support for NATO and his stepping back from the 'strategic ambiguity' over Taiwan.

Putin is a historical revisionist not only about Ukraine. He has also written a long essay arguing that the 1938 appeasement at Munich was the real start of the Second World War, not the Russian-Nazi pact of 1939.

Putin's invasion of Ukraine has in fact created a new hot *and* cold war. And his nuclear sabre-rattling has brought the world back to the darkest days of the first cold war. As the *Bulletin of Atomic Scientists* had indicated on its cover – the famous Armageddon clock is now 90 seconds to Doomsday. The Kremlin in February 2023 suspended Russia's participation in the new Strategic Arms Reduction Talks with the US (although Washington had been stalling too on a number of arms reductions and controls). In March 2023 Putin announced that he was putting tactical nuclear weapons in Belarus, the first time that Moscow had stationed nuclear weapons outside its own territory since 1995. On Russian TV, Putin said, 'The USA has been doing this for decades. They have long deployed their tactical nuclear weapons on the territory of its allied countries.' A fair point.

Behind the mask

Putin is famously secretive about his personal life and especially his family. That may be an issue of security or because of the habitual discreet style of his KGB background.

Putin has two daughters, Maria and Katerina, from his marriage to Lyudmila Shkrebneva. The couple first met in 1983 when she was working as a flight attendant and were together for thirty years as Putin quickly rose to the top of Russia's greasy pole.

But then, in 2008, a Russian newspaper (*Moskovsky Korrespondent*) reported that Putin had divorced Shkrebneva and was engaged to Olympic gold medal gymnast Alina Kabaeva, thirty years his junior. She came from a mixed Russian-Muslim Tatar parentage and had achieved great fame as a gymnast as well as scandal (because of doping charges). Putin denied the claims and the newspaper was shut down shortly after the report but he didn't publicly announce his divorce from Shkrebneva until five years later. Though the Kremlin continues to deny Putin's love affair with Kabaeva, they're believed to have four children together, including twins.

Despite the secrecy about this personal life, Putin has forged something of a national brand as a hunting-shooting-fishing outdoorsman. He has excelled in judo as a black belt and appears to perform well on the ice-hockey rink (though opponents are apparently told to go easy on him). He is populist in his rhetoric. Putin is renowned for his salty vocabulary, rather clipped delivery and uncompromising asides. Unafraid to employ earthy Russian street argot, he once threatened to wipe out Chechen rebels 'in the shithouse', and on another occasion – to press conference gasps and giggles – invited a journalist questioning Russia's tactics in Chechnya to come to Moscow 'to be circumcised' and then join the rebels. Putin does sometimes overdo the *gangsta* rap – when he just misses the beat of the street bad-boy lingo.

In terms of diplomatic language Putin is (justifiably) proud of his fluent German, said to have improved even further in recent years, thanks to his friendship with former German chancellor Gerhard Schröder. Though comfortable conducting political discussions one-to-one in German, diplomatic protocol requires the Russian leader to revert to his native language when aides are in attendance to ensure they understand. Putin has also been studying English while president, but it is said that the judo expert is still wrestling with English vowel sounds: he rarely speaks English in public, and never in a diplomatic setting. He did, however, woo the International Olympic Committee in heavily accented but convincing English when bidding for the winter Olympics in Sochi, and famously crooned the Fats Domino hit *Blueberry Hill* in English at a charity event. The man certainly has some chutzpah.

Chapter Five

Putin's Wars

Vladimir Putin inherited a military hotch-potch and a mosaic of conflicts. After the USSR officially dissolved on 25 December 1991, despite initial attempts to maintain some military unity as the 'Armed Forces of the Commonwealth of Independent States', each new republic generally took over control of military assets on its soil. In some cases, this was straightforward but with the big nuclear arsenals in Ukraine, for example, it was not. Kazakhstan and Belarus had also maintained nuclear weapons on their territories.

The Russian forces withdrew from eastern Europe without causing or witnessing bloodshed, although the exception – Romania – was a case of an unfinished revolution. The Ceausesçus were executed but the KGB was very involved in the succession. The Russian navy remained in its main base in Sevastopol in the Crimea and this caused disputes with the new Ukrainian government. Russian troops also remained in Abkhazia, South Ossetia and Transnistria.

When the USSR was dissolved it left more than 20 million ethnic Russians outside the boundaries of the Russian Federation. The Tsars had encouraged Russian settlement in newly conquered territories and the Bolsheviks took up the policy with zeal. So that left a patchwork of irredenta statelets all over Moscow's near abroad.

Transnistria

This was a largely Russian-speaking area that did not want to join the new Moldovan Republic. In November 1991, pro-Transnistrian militia were supported by elements of the Russian Fourteenth Army. On the other side stood the Moldovan army and police. On some occasions Russian troops openly backed the forces of the fledgling Transnistria republic. With intermittent ceasefires the conflict continued until July 1992.

The origins of the confrontation were partly historical as the west of the river Dniester (Nistru) was once part of Romania. The Molotov-Ribbentrop accord changed the geography here as it did in large parts of eastern Europe. Today's Transnistria was an autonomous part of the Ukrainian Soviet Socialist Republic but then the Moldovan SSR was heavily Russified in an intentional process of cultural separation from Romania. In the era of *perestroika*, many in this area wanted to re-join Romania. But in Transnistria, during the final days of the USSR, Russian and Ukrainian migrants outnumbered ethnic Moldovans.

Differences over language and even the alphabet (Roman versus Cyrillic) played a role in ethnic volatility as the Moldovan government did push hard to move from the Russian language and culture. Thus Transnistria became one of the so-called 'unrecognized republics' along with Abkhazia, South Ossetia and Nagorno-Karabakh.

Moldova set up its own army and deployed old Soviet weaponry as well as arms and advisors sent by Romania. But Russian forces in Transnistria numbered about 14,000 professional soldiers. The Kremlin encouraged the Transnistria capital of Tiraspol to seek independence.

Like many of the small wars inherited from the collapse of communism, the confrontation mixed very local ethnic issues. The large Ukrainian minority fought for Transnistria with pro-Russian separatists and it was sometimes described as 'a Slav battle against Moldovan-Romanian imperialism'. But the presence of the powerful Russian Fourteenth army made the Ruritanian victory of the Transnistria's possible. Nevertheless, about a thousand people, soldiers and civilians, died in this conflict. The stalemate between Moldova and Transnistria added profoundly to the many complications of the later war between the Kremlin and Kyiv.

Chechnya

In 1858, after decades of tough resistance, Chechnya was conquered by Russia. This followed the defeat of Imam Shamil, whose fighters had vowed to establish an Islamic state. During the chaos of the Russian revolution, the Chechens briefly secured independence. Germany's invasion brought renewed hope of freedom from the Soviet yoke. When the Second World War ended, Joseph Stalin sought vengeance by wholesale deportation of the Chechens, mainly to Siberia, in Operation LENTIL. At least a quarter of the half million men, women and children who were forced at gunpoint from their homes, died in transit or in the appalling conditions of their exile. They were allowed to return in 1957, after Stalin's death. Even when they returned they found some of their homes taken over by Russian immigrants and, worse, some of the gravestones of their dead had been used in building works. The Chechens had been thoroughly suppressed for over 200 years and suffered near-genocide and so much righteous anger had been stored up against Moscow.

When the USSR collapsed in 1991, the Chechens again declared independence. In 1994 the Russians bungled a poorly planned bid to regain control. They attacked, as they had in Afghanistan twenty-five years before, at Christmas time, to dilute Western protests or attention. Perhaps a tenth of the population was killed in the onslaught, especially in Grozny, the capital. David Loyn, of the BBC, observed, 'For the first time since the Second World War thousands of shells were fired into a city in a single day. The snipers of Sarajevo seemed almost gentlemanly by comparison.' The main resistance leader, General Aslan Maskhadov, who had enjoyed a distinguished career in the Soviet armed forces, fought well and hard. A former British army officer and co-founder of Frontline TV News, Vaughan Smith, commented on the widespread support that the Chechens gave Maskhadov, 'If you were a fighter, you didn't get a shag from the missus that night unless you killed a Russian.' Amid growing public concern in a Russia that had grasped at media freedoms, Moscow withdrew its forces after heavy losses. Chechnya achieved substantial autonomy but not full independence. It did not achieve stability either, as warlordism and organized crime proliferated. In August 1999, Chechen fighters crossed into the neighbouring Russian republic of Dagestan as part of a planned Islamic insurrection in the region. The following year the Russians blamed the Chechens for a series of explosions in

Moscow apartment blocks. Others, including ex-KGB officer Alexander Litvinenko (who was famously assassinated by radiation poisoning in London), suspected that the Russian security services had bombed them to create a pretext for war and the re-election of President Vladimir Putin in 2000.

The first Chechen war had resulted in a no-score draw. But the fighting had demoralized and humiliated the Russian army and the backlash against the decay of the Russian state and military contributed massively to the rise of the Putin dictatorship.

The new assertive president ordered a brutal campaign to re-conquer the rebel state. Putin used the Second Chechen War to stoke Russian xenophobia and to curb his critical domestic media. Western media had covered the First Chechen War, although reporting had been sporadic. Because of this coverage during the first war, Russia imposed a total ban on independent journalists in the second. In February 2000, the Russians captured and destroyed much of Grozny. This time, however, the Russians combined the reconstruction, especially in the capital, with gross violations of human rights. After 9/11, Putin projected his Chechnya adventures as part of the wider war on global jihadist terror to mute criticism from Washington and London. As John Pilger opined, 'Having demonstrated his ability to keep post-Soviet Russia under control, Putin was Washington's and London's man, and in return received *carte blanche* in troublesome Chechnya.' If the Cold War had not ended, the Chechens would probably have been armed by the West in the same way that the Afghan fighters had received support in the 1980s. Journalists covering the war generally admired the Chechens' courage in fighting the Russians but understood why their struggle had been sacrificed to the politics of the new world order.

Chechen rebels seized a Moscow theatre in October 2002 and held 800 people hostage; 120 of the hostages were killed when Russian troops stormed the building. Moscow then damned the Chechens for organising the siege at North Ossetia's Beslan school, which ended in a bloodbath. The fighting by dissident Islamic fighters continued against the pro-Moscow Chechen leader, Ramzan Kadyrov. The anti-Russian forces were still trying to widen the conflict to include the whole of the Caucasus, where a kaleidoscope of conflicts smouldered, not least in Georgia.

In the early days of the Chechen independence wars, Western journalists could gain access to the region, though it was dangerous. The BBC's Jeremy Bowen produced powerful television footage in 1995 and succinctly described in his memoirs the Stalingrad-like conditions in Grozny. Since Putin's crackdown, it became increasingly difficult for foreign journalists to operate freely in Chechnya. A few Russians were allowed entry, and they reported the war from the official Moscow standpoint. A brave exception was Anna Politkovskaya, who wrote for the independent *Novaya Gazeta*. She travelled to Chechnya thirty-nine times between 1999 and 2001.

In one of her despatches from near Grozny in November 1999, Politkovskaya wrote:

> Our losses are immeasurable as we let the army get out of hand and degenerate into anarchy. By allowing such a war to be fought in our own country, without any rules, not against terrorists but against those who hate their own bandits perhaps even more strongly than we do, we are the losers and the loss is irreversible.

Politkovskaya made many powerful enemies. In Chechnya, senior Russian officers repeatedly threatened her with rape. She survived numerous death threats and an attempted poisoning in 2004. Then, in October 2006, she was murdered in her Moscow apartment building. Experts suspect it was a contract killing.

In 2007 Putin declared the war to be over, but a secret partisan war was still underway. Conservative estimates were that 200,000 Chechens had been killed in the fighting since 1994. Officially, Moscow has admitted that 10,000 federal troops were killed in combat in Chechnya, which is certainly an underestimate. Of the approximately one million Russian troops who survived, many of the veterans became alcoholics, unemployable and anti-social, suffering from what has been termed 'the Chechen syndrome'.

By mid-2007 the Russians were using their Chechen loyalist proxies, some of whom had been bought, while others claimed to have been disenchanted with the small number of foreign Islamic extremists who had infiltrated and dominated the separatist forces. Many utterly war-weary Chechens hoped that Putin's strong-arm tactics, allied to reconstruction, would allow Ramzan Kadyrov, Moscow's man and certainly no bleeding-heart liberal, to bring peace of sorts. Better one warlord in control, they said, than several competing bandit or jihadist leaders.

Chechnya was only one of many largely hidden wars, places where most media couldn't reach. Tibet was closed to foreign correspondents, as was Burma, where the Karen people were being exterminated. The list of conflicts ignored in Africa was long. Sometimes the sheer inaccessibility of the fighting and the restrictions of authoritarian regimes deterred reporters. More often, though, it was a straightforward question of Western news values. To quote the intrepid Welsh correspondent, Jeremy Bowen, 'A traditional British newsroom follows a terrible arithmetic. Generally speaking, the further away from London, and the poorer the people, the more deaths it takes to qualify as a big story.'

The wars in the Balkans were extensively covered, partly because of the advent of lightweight cameras deployed by journalists as well as by ordinary citizens. This was a portent of the twentieth-first century phenomenon of citizen journalists armed with cameras in their mobile phones. Wars suddenly became more difficult to hide. And the inevitable atrocities were also hard to disguise as well.

The wars of Islamic extremism, from phone footage of the 7/7 attacks on the London Underground to the unofficial recording of Saddam Hussein's hanging, resulted in an explosion of images. These reports by amateurs were increasingly absorbed into mainstream news. They may have dramatized the stories but they may also have undermined the professionals' anxious search for context in the bewildering new world disorder.

The Russian army committed many atrocities in Afghanistan in the 1980s and in Putin's Chechen wars; few cameras were around to record them. But in the contemporary wars such as Ukraine nearly everyone had a mobile phone and could record the murders and rapes.

The Russian army had improved its performance in the Second Chechen War. It co-ordinated much better and had improved tactics and weapons, not least from its thermobaric arsenal. Instead of making the rebels fight to the death, many were encouraged to come 'on side' and survive; that was useful if it also satisfied the many tribal feuds. Ramzan Kadyrov, at 46, made the switch; he had fought against the Russians in the first war. Despite proclaiming his utmost loyalty to Putin and vociferously siding with him in the Ukraine War, the Chechen president had in effect grasped more autonomy in practice than in the previous 200 years. Putin has sometimes shown impatience with his unruly and mercurial ally. And probably a third Chechen war was likely but that would not suit Moscow while the Ukraine conflict raged.

The actual butcher's bill for the first war was around 5,500 dead from the Russian army and police; and perhaps 5,200 for the second round. These figures were no doubt understated. Although Russian and foreign journalists risked their lives to tell the harsh reality of the Chechen fighting, Putin had learned to control the narrative, not least by excluding all independent correspondents. Via more censorship and embedding house-trained journalists, Moscow re-fashioned the media narrative as patriotic professional soldiers defeating Chechen gangsters and jihadists. Putin also seemed genuinely offended that the West had rejected his version of the war in Chechnya as part and parcel of the war on terror. He hated the West damning his harsh but successful methods. But Putin also noted that

> the West stuck to stern words and diplomatic expressions of grave concern. He began to believe that, especially when faced with a fait accompli and tough rebuttal, for all the West's economic and, indeed, military might, it lacked one crucial strategic asset: will. That, he seems to have concluded, was Russia's strategic advantage.[1]

Hitler had also exaggerated the 'triumph of the will' and he, too, was proved wrong especially in the fighting in Ukraine and southern Russia.

And yet in the Second Chechen War Putin had successfully displayed what bold leadership could do. He made a point of visiting the front and denouncing the enemy: he promised to 'wipe out the terrorists and the bandits'.

Georgia on his mind

In August 2008, tensions with Georgia escalated into war after Georgian troops attacked Russian-backed separatist forces in South Ossetia. Russia then pushed Georgian forces from South Ossetia and Abkhazia, later recognizing them both as independent states.

The Republic of Georgia had declared its independence when the USSR fell apart (just as it had during the Russian revolution) while Russian troops backed the separatists. Moscow-Tbilisi relations had reached a crisis point by April 2008 when Georgia was seriously requesting NATO membership. Georgian government troops moved into a rebel stronghold in South Ossetia, while Russian troops retaliated and then Abkhaz forces opened a second front.

Although the conflict lasted just five days, it is sometimes considered the first European war of the twenty-first century and it was 'modern' in the sense that cyber warfare coincided with military action as well as an early use of drones. France, in the form of President Nicolas Sarkozy, negotiated a ceasefire in mid-August 2008 and it was firmed up by the visit of Condoleezza Rice, the US Secretary of State. Meanwhile the two new 'states' in Europe indulged in ethnic cleansing by pushing out Georgians – nearly 200,000 people were displaced while Tbilisi severed diplomatic relations with Moscow.

Many elements of the Russo-Georgian war were to be repeated later by Putin in Ukraine. For example, the 'passportization' policy laid the foundation for the Russian claims to the Georgian territory – Russian passports were handed out in large numbers in the separatist enclaves while Moscow supplied most of the separatist budget and made sure that Russians controlled the security police.

Georgia also had a colour revolution – just like Ukraine. In 2004 Mikheil Saakashvili came to power in the Rose Revolution that had ousted Eduard Shevardnadze, the last foreign minister of the USSR. The Kremlin had largely trusted this Georgian-born leader though he was considered a liberal, unlike Joseph Stalin (Dzhugashvili) who was considered Georgian through and through).

Saakashvili had promised to crush separatism as well as to join the EU and NATO. During the NATO summit in April 2008 in Bucharest, President George W. Bush campaigned to allow Georgia and Ukraine to join NATO via a MAP (Membership Action Plan). France and Germany opposed the American president saying that it would cause unnecessary offence to the Kremlin. 'What the West celebrated as a flowering of democracy the autocratic Putin saw as geopolitical and ideological encirclement', as Robert Kagan wrote in the *Washington Post* at the time.[2] Kagan added that the Russian invasion would be seen later as significant as the fall of the Berlin Wall. 'It marked the official return of history.' He also presciently compared it with the German invasion of Czechoslovakia in 1938.

Moscow played the Kosovo card – it did not want the former province of Serbia to be recognized by the West after NATO had intervened militarily in 1999. Moscow then switched tack and said it would recognize Abkhazia and South Ossetia if NATO went ahead and recognized Kosovo. Georgia had no major oil or gas reserves but it was in a crucial strategic position next to Turkey and Iran and it hosted part of the Baku-Tbilisi-Ceyhan pipeline supplying oil to NATO member Turkey.

There is little argument that the invasion of Georgia led the way to the incursions and then major invasion into Ukraine. The same tactics were employed: big Russian military exercises and then attacking civilian targets, especially in Gori. Ethnic Georgians fleeing from South Ossetia were told by Russian troops: 'Putin has given an order that everyone must be either shot or forced to leave.' Accusations of war crimes proliferated.

Naval assaults were conducted by the Black Sea Fleet from Sevastopol on the 190 miles of Georgian coastline – their first real engagements since 1945. The Russians briefly occupied the crucial port of Poti and the Russian army came within thirty miles of the capital, Tbilisi – obviously with the threat of a decapitation plan and regime change. Soon the recognition of the breakaway statelets ensued. Putin claimed that he was protecting Russian speakers abroad – this was *Civis Romanus Sum* writ large.

Georgia had sent initially seventy troops, including medics, to fight alongside the coalition in the 2003 Operation IRAQI FREEDOM; the number was dramatically increased to win Washington's approval. It went up to 2,300 Georgian military personnel; there were also Georgians serving in a separate UN Mission. The Americans also provided equipment and conducted extensive training of the Georgian armed forces, much to the distaste of Putin. President Saakashvili impulsively overplayed his hand – he assumed (wrongly) NATO or certainly the Americans would protect him if the Russians stepped in. Washington had warned him that his confidence was misplaced. During the war a desperate Georgian president had to beg Washington to rapidly return his combat troops serving in Iraq. What had started as a surgical strike to take back two enclaves became a fight for the country's very survival as the Russians kept advancing.

Despite US assistance the Georgians fought badly in their five-day war – no air power that worked, nor navy. The Russians were also poorly co-ordinated – they did not establish air supremacy despite the fact that no Georgian fighter aircraft were evident in opposition, though some of its old Soviet and new Israeli SAMs worked. Like the Second Chechen war, Russians fought with largely professional soldiers, but it was obviously still a big army with far less proficiency than NATO forces. During the crossing of the mountains into Georgia, Russian commanders had to borrow phones from journalists.

Nearly 850 people were killed in the short war, while some 35,000 Georgians were left homeless. By not backing Georgia's defence the international community, especially NATO, had proved to the Russians that it was essentially lacking the will to put its power where it put its fine words. If Putin let Georgia go West, then who would be next? As Russia expert Mark Galeotti said in 2018, 'In hindsight, one wonders would the Crimea and Donbas wars have happened if the West had been more robust in its response to Georgia?'

The intervention in Syria

Putin felt that the West had hoodwinked him over the NATO intervention in Libya. In Syria he would go in but cautiously and with small increments of power. After all, the Syrian government was a long-term ally of Moscow and it needed help in a hell-brew of a complex hydra-headed war. Also, the Russians had previously worked closely with the Syrian military.

In 2015 the Kremlin intervened in the Syrian civil war, at the request of the beleaguered President al-Assad. Damascus granted the Russians the free use of the Basel al-Assad airbase (which the Russians called Hmeymim) that was forty miles north of Moscow's small naval facility at Tartus. Russian air sorties soon started hammering the Islamic State, which had seized large parts of the Syria and Iraq.[3] The Russians were also hitting the Free Syrian Army and other groups that were backed by the Americans. The Russians wanted to show that they could help their Syrian allies, who had been reduced to controlling only about 10 per cent of the country. Russian stand-off power – bombs and missiles – were also there to warn off the West. As well as air power, the Russians deployed some of the vast array of artillery, with Russian officers and Syrian crews.

Moscow considered the intervention a success. The government recovered much of its territory, Islamic State was defeated, Turkish-backed forces were confined to the north and only small areas around Idlib were controlled by anti-Assad rebels. The Americans too had left, deserting their Kurdish allies who had fought so hard against the Islamists.

Barack Obama had warned that chemical weapons were a red line. But Washington misjudged Putin when Assad did use chemical weapons against his own citizens. But after British MPs refused in the House of Commons to back Prime Minister David Cameron's call for the UK to get involved in Syria, the US president said he would leave it to Congress to decide whether to enter the war. 'We were open-jawed and dumbfounded,' said the US ambassador to Syria, Robert Ford, who was expecting immediate air strikes. At the G20 summit in St Petersburg in September 2013 Obama accepted an offer to play peacemaker by persuading Assad to give up chemical weapons in return for dropping the idea of air strikes. Obama later said that it was 'one of the decisions I am most proud of'. But not punishing the crossing of the red line taught Putin what he thought he or his allies could get away with.

The Israelis who had had maintained good relations with Moscow, kept up their on-off fight with Hezbollah and the Iranian Revolutionary Guards in Syria. Jerusalem would notify the Russian air force which would switch off their air defence systems to avoid any conflict with Israel. The Russians had also developed a complex deconfliction system with the Americans to avoid direct dogfights.

Russia secured air bases and a confirmed a port as well as shoring up a key ally. The Kremlin was once more a big player in the Middle East, while Washington was again challenged in the region. The eastern Med became a frequent location for Russian warships. The war had also been a testbed for new weapons and techniques for the Russians.

Some of the lessons may have been wrongly applied, especially in Ukraine. About 7,000 soldiers were deployed (including some 2,500 Wagner men at the peak), albeit in regular rotation. Wagner forces were used rather carelessly in the first recovery of the wonderful Palmyra ruins that IS troops had shamefully desecrated. Perhaps only 100 Spetsnaz were involved, as forward air controllers and artillery advisers as well as snipers. Moscow drew a lesson that a fairly small force could achieve a lot, especially if the Americans kept out of the picture. Sure, Barack Obama had almost entered the fray fully when chemical weapons were used by the Syrians. And even the anti-interventionist Donald Trump sent a token array of missiles. Generally, however, Moscow had shored up its ally, had swaggered on the Middle Eastern stage and seen off a half-hearted USA. This was the wrong lesson to be applied to Ukraine, however.

Presidents Erdoğan and Putin were autocrats who often seemed cut from the same cloth. But in November 2015 a Turkish F-16 brought down a Russian Su-24 bomber with a missile. Moscow clamped sanctions briefly on Istanbul but soon fences were mended. Despite being a member of NATO, with the second largest army, it has felt an outsider. Partly because the EU doesn't want a large Muslim country to join. The common view in Turkey is that the Europeans are happy for Turks to fight for them, work for them, but not keen on Turkey to join them. That sense of alienation suits Putin who has used Erdoğan as an intermediary with the West, especially over the Ukraine war. In addition, Turkish control of the Dardanelles gives them a chokehold over Russia's navy in the Black Sea.

Other entanglements

Russia's invasion of Ukraine had made life more difficult for Azerbaijan, Armenia and Georgia. They have wanted to balance Russian leverage with a desire to support Ukrainian sovereignty. Russia plays an important role in the most volatile conflict in the region – the fight between Armenia and Azerbaijan over Nagorno-Karabakh. Despite Russian peacekeepers, the decades-long war over the breakaway, primarily ethnic Armenian, region in Azerbaijan flared up again in 2020, causing more than 1,000 casualties.

Armenia is a member of the Russia-led Collective Security Treaty Organization (CSTO). Yet it was Russian arms sales to Azerbaijan that helped Baku to capture territory in the 2020 war. But Moscow has negotiated various ceasefires and Russian peacekeepers are stationed in Azerbaijan territory. But Azerbaijan has a strong ties with Ukraine which has backed Azerbaijan's claim to the disputed enclave. Azerbaijan has been sending very cheap fuel to Kyiv. Armenia hosts over 10,000 Russian troops including a big Russian base. Armenia also wants to maintain ties with the EU and the West but does not support Kyiv because of its previous support for Azerbaijan.

Georgia meantime knows that popular sentiment favours Ukraine and pro-Kyiv demonstrators have often taken to the streets, but the Georgian government has to tread carefully after the hammering it got from Russia in the 2008 war.

The complex legacy of the collapse of the USSR will continue to complicate Russia's foreign and defence policy for years and decades to come, even if the Ukraine crisis is magically resolved tomorrow.

Chapter Six

The Blame Game

The Big Hurt

It is often forgotten in the West how much the Russians suffered in previous invasions, especially by the Third Reich. The USA had been a crucial ally then but, in Russian eyes, it became a real threat during the Cold War. Next came the hubristic triumphalism of Washington when the USSR broke up. NATO launched its first ever no-fly zone over Bosnia and US planes shot down four Bosnian Serb warplanes; then the 'peaceful alliance' conducted hundreds of air strikes in 1994 and 1995. NATO's war against Serbia was even more aggressive in 1999 over Kosovo's independence. Even the Chinese embassy in Belgrade was bombed by NATO planes. Finally, the invasions of Iraq and Afghanistan convinced many Russians that the claims that NATO was a defensive alliance were not credible.

One of the best summaries of this Russian perception is by an acute British observer, the former UK ambassador to Moscow, Rodric Braithwaite:

> All this left a very bitter taste in Russian mouths. Many Russians who had seen America as a model for decades now lost their belief in Western good faith and were convinced that their country had been deliberately brought low and humiliated not by its own weaknesses but by the intrigues of domestic traitors and foreign spies. Nostalgic for the days when their country was the other superpower, they concluded that Western ideas about democracy were wholly unsuited for Russia, and retreated into an unpleasant, sickly and defiant nationalism. The West never understood why.[1]

The Russian revolution had promised their grandparents and parents a glittering future and they had won the Great Patriotic War against all the odds but then, in 1991, it all collapsed and starvation stalked the land again. What had gone wrong? The old questions returned about the nature of Russian history and the innate character of the people. The Germans had encountered the same self-searching malaise after 1945 but they had been totally defeated, and their conquerors and, in some cases, their own consciences, had forced them to face not only their democratic failures but their many massive war crimes. The Russians had won their war and did not feel as though they had lost the Cold War. The Germans were not allowed to support Nazism after May 1945 but many Russians still clung to their belief in communism, if not always the Communist Party. There was no official de-Stalinisation.

Ukraine as a red line

Ukraine, along with Belarus, had been considered part of Russia for over a thousand years. Most Russians regarded the inhabitants of these neighbouring countries as brothers or, at least, cousins and certainly they were fellow Slavs sharing the same culture and similar languages. Russia faced much angst when Kyiv broke away in 1991 but the new independent Ukrainian government did not push its luck by preventing Russian use of the major naval base in Crimea.

Who then was to blame for the first outbreak of major war in Europe since 1945? To be sure, Russia invaded on a massive scale in February 2022 and then committed serious war crimes, not least the capture and removal of thousands of Ukrainian children, the war crime for which Putin was indicted at the International Criminal Court. And the only one that the Russians did not deny. And yet many Russian securocrats felt that their country was facing an existential threat as NATO kept driving across red lines that defended fundamental Russian national interests.

The case for the defence – Putin's perspective.

As I write this sentence, 30 May 2023, a fleet of drone-bombers was striking Moscow, hitting residential apartment blocks – that is, civilian areas. It was assumed that the attacks came from Ukraine. Washington immediately distanced itself and said that America had actively discouraged Kyiv from taking the war to Russian soil. London was more nuanced and said that Ukraine had the right of self-defence but insisted that no longer-range UK weapons were involved. Along with Ukrainian-backed insurgent groups crossing the borders to hit Russian towns and now drone attacks on Moscow, the possibility of full-scale war, even nuclear conflict, loomed larger; especially after Ukraine began its long-heralded counter-offensive on 4 June 2023.

The Kremlin warned that initial humanitarian aid to Ukraine would escalate to direct attempts by NATO to degrade Russian military capability. Washington's policy would lead to many Ukrainians and Russians dying. From this emerged the ironic comment that the West would fight to the last Ukrainian to preserve Ukrainian sovereignty.

The prosecution case is clear:

1. NATO expanded more than a thousand miles eastwards, after achieving the re-unification of Germany. NATO conducted numerous military exercises near the Russian border.
2. NATO was not a defensive alliance but an aggressive one. Moscow would list the invasions of Afghanistan, Iraq and the attacks on Libya. The Kremlin was especially sensitive about the NATO attack on Serbia (a long-term Slav ally) and the backing of Kosovo independence.
3. Washington had withdrawn, after thirty years, from the anti-ballistic missile treaty signed by Leonid Brezhnev and Richard Nixon in 1972. Trump also withdrew from the Intermediate Range Nuclear Force Treaty, a deal that had been signed by Ronald Reagan and Mikhail Gorbachev (the final leader of the USSR) that helped to remove nearly 3,000 missiles and allowed effective on-site inspection.

Zelensky in liberated Kherson. (*Official Ukraine*)

Vladimir Putin with Valery Gerasimov (left) and Sergei Shoigu (right). (*Russian government*)

Alexei Navalny.

Alina Kabaeva.

Yevgeny Prigozhin.

Minister of Defence Sergei Shoigu. (*Official photo*)

Oleskandr Syrskyi, Colonel General Ukraine forces. (*Ukraine MoD*)

Anna Politkovska. (*Wikipedia*)

Mikhail Khodorkovsky. (*Times of Moscow*)

Dmitry Utkin. (*Passport picture, Wikipedia*)

Elon Musk marketing a flame-thrower. (*Techradar*)

Russian tanks near Kyiv.

Centre of Kyiv. (*Author*)

War museum near Kyiv displaying Soviet Mi24. (*Author*)

HIMARS artillery. (*US Department of Defense*)

Ukrainian tractor pulling away Russian tank meme.

Possibly the real thing (another meme).

US troops training with South Koreans. (*DoD*)

Sheltering from the bombing in Kharkiv.

Russian MiG 29.

Russian cruiser *Moskva*. (*Russian navy*)

Ukrainian navy drone.

War damage in Mariupol.

Mariupol ruins.

May Day parade Moscow 2022.

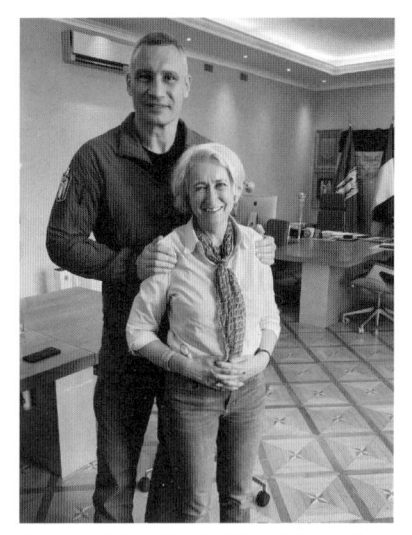

Mayor of Kyiv Vitaly Klitschko with British reporter Lindsey Hilsum, 2023.

Boxers with official emblem – many bad taste patriotic items were sold.

Ukrainian tank.

F-16. Can a 50-year-old plane turn the tide of the war? (*Lockheed Martin*)

The Russians flooded the Kakhovka Dam on 6 June 2023.

Can the German Leopard change the balance on land?

Putin balloon joke.

Umm Qasr, Iraq. Allied bombing in 2003. (*Author*)

Zaporizhzhia, Europe's biggest nuclear power station.

Abrahams M1A1, Baghdad. (*Tim Lambon*)

Afghan War. Knocked-out Russian armour near Kabul, 1984 (author top right).

Author testing weapons with Ukrainian army, near Kyiv.

German NATO troops in Kabul in 2002. (*Author*)

War damage in Kyiv.

Ukrainian Bayrakter drone. (*Ukraine ministry of defence*)

Armata tank concept design.

Ukrainians troops in early fight back near Kyiv.

US B-2 Spirit stealth bomber. (*US DoD*)

UK GCHQ in Cheltenham. (*UK MoD*)

Korean end game. Korean War Memorial Washington DC. (*Author*)

4. Washington actively encouraged a right-wing anti-Russian coup in Kyiv in 2014.
5. The American government also actively encouraged Kyiv to become a member of NATO and the EU, even though if Washington had declared Ukraine could *not* join NATO for a very long time (the unvarnished truth) it could perhaps have averted war. The 'Finlandization' of Ukraine could once have worked. The Kremlin had respected the neutrality of Austria in the early post-war period, and Finland's neutrality was later respected as well. Instead, US training had brought up Ukrainian forces almost to the NATO standards even before Kyiv got anywhere near joining the alliance. And then provided much more modern lethal weapons, including, finally, the F-16 fighter jets.
6. Washington constantly backed Kyiv's hard-line stance against Russia and this prevented peace deals and led inexorably to the Russian military blowback.

That is the essence of the case for the Kremlin. So, to consider this argument in more detail.

The West denies it now but Gorbachev refused to use force in Germany (unlike in Lithuania) but instead he pulled out 400,000 Soviet troops and some intelligence agents (including Putin) on the understanding that not only would a unified Germany not join NATO but also the alliance would not expand into former Warsaw Pact countries. This is not Russian propaganda but based on numerous high-level personal assurances from Western leaders. There is no single written treaty, however. Numerous Russian experts – not necessarily friends of Putin – have insisted they were told in lots of smoky backrooms that NATO would stop expanding now that German unification had arrived. The previous reunification of Germany in the late 1930s had caused the 1939–45 war. And the whole panoply of West European policy thereafter had been to 'keep America in, Russia out and Germany down'. Western politicians such as Margaret Thatcher were often more hostile to German unity than many Russians.

On 9 February 1990 the US Secretary of State, James Baker, met Gorbachev and publicly and famously promised 'not one inch eastward'. One of many American promises unkept.

The lack of faith after German unification was the original sin and the beginning of the Kremlin mantra that the American leaders could not be trusted to tell the truth about what they were planning for Europe. The suspicions were confirmed in 1999 when three new countries, the Czech Republic, Hungary and especially Poland, joined NATO. The Poles had a very long history of fighting, and sometimes beating, the Russians. The NATO border moved 400 miles eastwards in the direction of Russia at a time when Russia's economy was spluttering towards a standstill. Then NATO expanded again in 2004, including Estonia which had a 183-mile border with Russia. Russian generals used to grimace and joke that the American invaders could catch a local bus to St Petersburg. NATO had now expanded over 1,000 miles to nudge up against the Russian Federation.

In 2008 at the NATO summit in Bucharest, the future membership of Ukraine and Georgia was announced, though no formal action was undertaken to start the process. Ukraine and Russia then shared a 1,200-mile border, parts of which are just 400 miles from Moscow. The US ambassador to Moscow, William J. Burns, sent a famous cable to Washington which said 'Nyet Means Nyet'. He emphasized the Russian fear of encirclement and that Ukraine and Georgia were definitely clear red lines.

Four months after the NATO announcement, Russia launched its five-day war with Georgia just days after a large joint US Army-Georgian Army training exercise inside Georgia. Over 2,000 US troops had been involved.

An immediate *casus belli* in Ukraine was the US backing for the coup in Kyiv in 2014 which forced the democratically elected pro-Russian president to flee the country. As Professor John Mearsheimer, at the University of Chicago, explained at the time:

The new government in Kiev was pro-Western and anti-Russian to the core. And it contained four high-ranking members who could legitimately be labelled neo-fascists.[2]

Washington continued to pour arms into Ukraine, arguing for NATO inter-operability even though it was not a member of the alliance. The US always claimed those were defensive arms such as body armour but later the equipment became more offensive-orientated. NATO also built up new missile systems in Romania and Poland. In Romania the Mark-41 Aegis missile launchers were dubbed defensive ABMs but they could also fire nuclear-tipped missiles capable of hitting Moscow. The Aegis system was originally devised for naval warfare; then Lockheed Martin developed a land-based version that was installed in Romania in 2016 and later planned for Poland but that project was stood down. The Kremlin did not buy the US argument that the systems were defensive and concerned with missiles coming from Iran and North Korea.

Russian military thinkers had genuine anxieties that NATO expansion and new missile systems along Russia's borders could, in extremis, hand Washington a major strategic advantage and opportunity to launch a first strike against Russian command-and-control systems.

In July 2021 NATO held a large naval exercise in the Black Sea region, involving thirty-two navies; Operation SEA BREEZE almost led to the Russian navy firing on a British destroyer that entered what Moscow considered its territorial waters. Brussels announced that the exercise was especially important since Russia's annexation of the Crimea. NATO HQ said that the exercise was co-hosted by the US Navy's Sixth Fleet and the Ukrainian navy; the exercise would focus on 'multiple warfare areas including amphibious warfare, land manoeuvre warfare, diving operations, maritime interdiction operations, air defence, special operations integration, anti-submarine warfare, and search and rescue operations'. Pretty comprehensive then.

In 2020 and 2021 NATO conducted live-fire training exercises using missiles inside Estonia, just seventy miles from the Russian border. Meanwhile, Washington re-affirmed its commitment to Ukraine joining

NATO by signing a number of bilateral security arrangements. Bilateral deals and nearly forty NATO interoperability exercises looked very sinister from Moscow's perspective. Moscow kept warning Washington. In December 2021, Sergey Lavrov, Russia's foreign minister, said publicly: 'We reached our boiling point.' The Kremlin continued to demand a written guarantee that Ukraine would never become part of NATO.

The Kremlin asked repeatedly how Washington would respond if Moscow (or Beijing) established a military alliance with Canada or Mexico and installed Russian missiles just seventy miles from the US border and then undertook numerous live-fire exercises? The actual historical example, Cuba 1962, showed that the two countries went to the edge of nuclear war. The US had the Monroe doctrine and the Kremlin kept trying to explain that Ukraine was part of Russia's equivalent of the Monroe doctrine. Geographic proximity is part of the American way of defence, so why should Washington not understand the Kremlin's similar sensitivities?

Many Western experts, including hawks, have long warned of the over-extension of NATO. Even George Kennan, the famous father of Soviet containment, as a 94-year-old sage, said that the NATO expansion 'would make the Founding Fathers turn in their graves'. The original NATO had been about fighting expansionist Soviet communism, and that had almost completely evaporated. Kennan had served as US ambassador to Moscow and understood the Russians. Perhaps he was the most influential diplomat of the twentieth century. He lived for more than a century, more than long enough to see his creation – NATO – turn in on itself; his final conclusion on NATO expansion was that it was 'a strategic blunder of potentially epic proportions'.

Convinced Russophobes, however, also warned that NATO's land grabs were dangerous. Other critics simply said that Putin would try to 'wreck' Ukraine if Kyiv got close to joining the Brussels-based alliance, just as he had dismembered Georgia. Other hawks, of course, wanted to do everything to undermine Moscow at any price because they saw Putin as an insane Hitler Mark 2. Russian encroachments into Ukraine were simply irrational Russian revanchism and old-time nationalism. Those worse-case planners in the Pentagon who gamed a possible first strike against Moscow may have held similar views although, as in all militaries, senior officers are always tasked with thinking the unthinkable.

Those who espoused expansion now argue that Russia's invasion proved they were right all along, not that their policy had a causal effect on the Kremlin. The followers of Kennan said that the expansion would create a self-fulfilling prophecy and lead to war between the old rivals. First a proxy war and then a real war.

Chapter Seven

The Road to War

It was much easier for Washington to inflict sanctions on Russia but the energy-dependent EU states would suffer extensively from the blowback. An economic campaign could easily be upset by military events, however. And it was. Tragically, the downing of MH17 was a major factor in refashioning the political dynamics against the Kremlin. Malaysian Airlines Flight 17, a scheduled passenger flight from Amsterdam to Kuala Lumpur, was brought down by a Buk 9M36 anti-aircraft missile under Russian-controlled forces. It was shot down on 17 July 2014 while flying over eastern Ukraine; all 298 passengers and crew were killed. The missile system had been transported from the Russian Federation on the day of the crash and then the launch system was returned to Russia soon afterwards. Later, Dutch-led detailed inquiries confirmed initial German, American and Ukrainian intelligence sources. Russia denied all involvement though its version has varied over time.

On 25 July 2014 the EU expanded its list of sanctioned Russian individuals and companies but, more significantly, it followed the American lead in limiting Russian financial institutions' access to capital markets. The tensions were not just financial; Russian air force brinkmanship led to very close near misses between Russian jets and Western aircraft, both civilian and military. The most dangerous example was when a Russian SU-27 Flanker flew very close to an American RC-135 reconnaissance aircraft in international airspace over the Baltic Sea.

Western sanctions were supposed to weaken the Russian economy and so turn Russians against their government. Instead, the Ukraine crisis appeared to galvanize the majority of Russians *against* the West, not the Kremlin. Hostility to the EU and America grew as the Kremlin leveraged the threat perception to boost its domestic support.

Ukraine, too, was under economic pressure. The Kyiv government launched a fresh round of privatization as public services were cut as part of an $40 million International Monetary Fund bailout. Pensions were reduced as were government-funded salaries. Healthcare facilities were reduced and half the universities were closed, even though Ukraine had an international reputation for good universities and during Soviet times attracted many international students especially from what was then called 'The Third World'.

The usually proffered solution was EU accession but that seemed to be a mirage as endemic corruption and ethnic disintegration caused by the civil war prompted Brussels to warn that membership could be twenty-five years away. Meanwhile, legislation about the promised elections in the breakaway republics, as agreed at the Minsk protocols, never passed completely through the Kyiv parliament. Eventually, the separatist republics went their own way with elections in 2016 and 2018 that were not internationally recognized. Meanwhile, in contradiction of the same protocols, so-called 'non-lethal' military aid poured into Kyiv from the US while hundreds of military trainers came from the US and, later, other NATO states.

Minsk 1 and 2 had achieved much in reducing military conflicts; after 2018 more civilians were killed by landmines and unexploded ordnance than by active hostilities. But the path to peace was devastated by political and diplomatic failures on both sides. Russia was accused of aggression and Washington sometimes appeared to be more intent on blaming the Kremlin rather than seriously trying to resolve the civil war. Covert NATO bases were built up in western Ukraine to allow NATO trainers to operate and the Ukrainian navy was also secretly enhanced.

Western special forces, including the SAS, were active too in training and observation roles. The Ukrainian army did not do so well in the first round of Russian incursions in 2014; NATO was determined this would not happen again.

A future war with Russia?

Now that major war has broken out again in Europe, it is sometimes forgotten what the mood in pre-war eastern Europe was like. Ukraine was a running sore, yes, but NATO planners were transfixed by the dangers posed by a Russian takeover in the small Baltic states; nobody in Brussels really thought that Russia would try to swallow the vast expanse of Ukraine.

After a successful year of fighting in Syria – namely saving President Assad from collapse – by the end of 2016 Putin looked as if he were on a roll. An admirer, Donald Trump, had even been elected US commander in chief. Putin was accused of deploying Russian cyber-power to hack into the emails of Trump's Democratic Party rival, Hillary Clinton, as well as other senior Democrats. Moscow had also improved relations with key Western allies in Egypt, Turkey and even Israel. Moscow started to plan joint naval patrols with the Chinese and then raised the stakes by talking about restoring bases in traditional allies' countries, such as Cuba and Vietnam.

Before the advent of Donald Trump, it looked almost as if Moscow and Washington were sleepwalking towards a shooting war. Sir John Sawyers was the head of Britain's Secret Intelligence Service (SIS), more commonly known as MI6. He warned:

> We are moving into an era that is as dangerous, if not more dangerous, as the Cold War because we do not have that focus on a strategic relationship between Moscow and Washington.

The old protocols of deterrence had been lost. They were not speaking the same diplomatic language anymore. MAD, or Mutually Assured Destruction, had been fully understood, and feared, by both initial superpowers. Then China created a triangle. The diplomatic dance became more complicated when rogue states such as North Korea went nuclear. Nevertheless, from Moscow's first nuclear test in 1949 until the collapse of the Soviet Union, the language of mutual deterrence had been fully comprehensible, especially during the eyeball-to-eyeball Cuban missile crisis of 1962. After the Berlin Wall was torn down and the USSR dissolved, the Russian Federation maintained most of its nuclear arsenal. In the Budapest Memorandum of 1994, however, Ukraine agreed to give up its nukes – it had the world's third largest stockpile – in exchange for guarantees of its territorial integrity and independence. Belarus and Kazakhstan signed the same protocols which were guaranteed by Russia, the USA and the UK. France and China signed rather more evasive guarantees. When, in pre-2022, NATO members looked at Russia's covert invasion of large parts of Ukraine, they sighed and said under their breath: 'Thank God, Ukraine is not in NATO or we might have to defend it under article 5.' Yet, it could be argued that under the Budapest Memorandum at least America and the UK were obliged to defend *all* of Ukraine. Neither Washington nor London would do much more than send in a few infantry weapons and trainers to avoid inciting Moscow to seize all of eastern Ukraine.

The crisis in Ukraine was testing the mettle of the West. Even a presumed accident, when a Russian anti-aircraft system was sent to rebel-controlled Ukraine and returned within twenty-four hours, could have provoked a very major European crisis when Flight MH17 was shot down with 298 passengers and crew on board. NATO was not treaty-bound to engage in Ukraine but it definitely was in the three very nervous Baltic countries. Would Putin trade on the weakness and disunity in the West and chance his arm by a swift move into the Baltics? Logic dictated that he should consolidate his position in Ukraine before moving on the Baltics or even into non-NATO states such as Moldova. Putin, however, was rewriting the international order, both in Europe and in the Middle East. The massive migrant crisis connected the two, not always accidentally. Moscow could only benefit from the turmoil in the EU as populism and immigration swamped the attention of the Brussels elites.

What was the mood in the Baltic states? Over one million ethnic Russians lived in the three small countries with equally small populations, especially in the cities. Lithuania had around 5 per cent, while Latvia had 27 per cent and Estonia 24 per cent, according to a recent census.

Some Russians, and Russian speakers as a mother tongue, felt genuinely estranged by what they regarded as official discrimination but not all of them wanted Russia to intervene. Many enjoyed the freedoms that Estonia, Latvia and Lithuania had to offer as EU members, not least to travel and work throughout Europe. Many of the 'Russians' tended to live in the cities. In Riga, the Latvian capital, around 50 per cent were native Russian speakers. Riga had also elected the first ethnic Russian mayor since independence.

One way to gauge how the vast majority of *non*-Russian inhabitants felt about being ruled once more by Moscow is to visit the former KGB headquarters in Lukiškės Square in the centre of the Lithuanian capital of Vilnius. It is an imposing neo-classical building with thick walls that were useful for absorbing the screams from the many previous torture victims. Thousands of Lithuanians were shot there. It is now called the Museum of Genocide Victims and it describes how a third of the country's population were killed or deported to Siberia, courtesy of their Soviet liberators who had driven out the Nazis. The Germans used the building as an HQ in the Great War and then the Gestapo took it over in the second great conflagration. In the museums and school textbooks in the three states they all seem rather coy about how many local inhabitants shared the Nazi hatred of the Jews and failed usually to describe the large number of often eager recruits to the *Wehrmacht* or SS.

Just like young Israeli conscripts who are taken to Yad Vashem, the Holocaust Museum in Jerusalem, so too young Lithuanian soldiers are taken to see the barbarities of Russian rule. The Baltic states have endured a very short but cruel history. The non-Russians would fight hard against a Russian invasion but they could not do so without help.

Moving into the Baltics would prompt direct war with NATO. Such an outcome partly depends on the old Marxist term – 'the correlation of forces'. After the collapse of the USSR, the nuclear arsenal provided the crutch for dramatically deteriorating Russian conventional forces. By definition, this reduced the threshold at which Russia would consider the use of nuclear weapons. Russian military strategists talked more openly about the usability of nuclear weapons, as the Americans had in the

Dr Strangelove era of the 1950s and 1960s, not least because of the works of Henry Kissinger, who is satirized in the film. One Russian hawk talked publicly of 'reducing the US to nuclear ash'. Conversely and paradoxically, Putin's massive (attempted) revitalization of his conventional military capability could have the advantage of *raising* the nuclear threshold. Equally, the major decline in both American conventional commitments in place, as well as languid European defence spending pre-2022, meant that NATO might have to resort to doomsday weapons sooner rather than later if a shooting war broke out with Russia. Or just surrender.

Pre-2022 NATO members wondered whether Putin was mad enough to swallow the Baltics, which it was originally thought he could have done in months if not weeks. Or was it all a bluff? Appearing slightly crazy can be useful in terms of military deterrence. It is conventional wisdom that North Vietnam waited for the departure of Richard Nixon, prompted by Watergate in 1974, before they overtly invaded the south. They thought that the domestically besieged Nixon might be dangerous enough to throw everything at them for breaking the Paris Accords (and meanwhile looking tough to disenchanted American voters). Likewise, it was often said that French nukes had more credibility because President Charles de Gaulle was belligerent and curmudgeonly enough actually to use them. And today the great leader in North Korea may well be mad and bad enough to fire his nukes, if truly threatened.

Whatever his clinical state of mind – and Putin did not appear to be in even the same hospital let alone psychiatric ward as Nixon or Kim Jong-un or, arguably, Donald Trump – the Baltic governments were extremely worried even before 2022. Lithuania reinstated conscription. It also issued three updated survival guides after 2014. The last version is a seventy-five-page pamphlet offering advice on how to recognize friendly militaries and how to deal with unfriendly nuclear or chemical attacks. The Latvian national guard had been on constant red alert and many kept their weapons at home in readiness for the attack they feared was imminent. Estonia had hidden a thousand large survival capsules in their forests with supplies to support two years of guerrilla resistance. Noir dramas about Russian occupation played on Scandinavian TV.

Russian media started showing civil defence preparations and old nuclear bunkers. And, in a sad display of British impotence, Boris Johnson, the then UK foreign secretary, declared that people should protest outside the Russian embassy in London. That would strike fear in the heart of Putin, obviously. *One* solitary protestor with a single placard turned up. Most successful leaders know when to stop. Many warlords, however, display hubris, or overreach as it is now called. Hitler was the classic example, though he was probably insane. Appeasement, that noble flowering of liberal thought and logical legacy of millions of dead in the trenches, would have worked with a *rational* German leader. Would appeasement work better with Putin or was he the classic bully of Western media characterization who had to be confronted?

If Russian forces drove over the border into the Baltics, swamping the three small countries in days perhaps, it would have presented NATO with an existential threat to the organization and the West. If, at the beginning of the inevitably swift invasion, the diverse national ambassadors to NATO actually managed to agree on the declaration of Article 5 – 'the one for all and all for one clause' – as happened after the abomination of the onslaught on the Twin Towers, then what? Victory in Cold War Mark 1 depended on the belief that America would save its European allies. To recapture the Baltics would require a replay of Operations OVERLORD plus DESERT STORM. Such a conventional assault, assuming NATO could eventually summon the will and capability, could go nuclear. In the 1960s Charles de Gaulle never thought that the US would risk sacrificing Washington to defend Paris. Trumpian Washington had increasingly disengaged from an alliance which had become one huge welfare state, where America carried over 70 per cent of the load; the European states were largely freeloaders and dole-merchants who scrounged from the system. But Trump's screaming and shouting departure from the White House and the Ukraine war's gory arrival changed all that.

Novels often got closer to the truth than official histories. A former NATO deputy commander, General Sir Richard Shirreff, wrote a controversial novel called *2017: War with Russia*. This was only a slightly dramatized version of intelligence dossiers and war games that amounted to a *cri de coeur* about Western, especially British, defence cuts. In the novel, Russia invaded Latvia, Estonia and Lithuania after stirring up the Russian minorities and then paralyzed NATO by threatening to launch nukes. Shirreff's point was whether the West could pre-empt invasion by putting sufficient conventional defence forces into the Baltics or in nearby Poland. The British general rammed home his point by explaining why the biggest ship ever built for the Royal Navy, the *Queen Elizabeth* aircraft carrier, was sunk because it had no on-board fighter aircraft, or accompanying maritime surveillance planes, or enough escorts, both surface and underwater.

The foreword of the book was written by Admiral James Stavridis, the senior US naval officer who was former Supreme Allied Commander Europe. He said, 'I would put Russia right now as the number one threat … . Russia is the only country on earth that retains a nuclear capability to destroy the United States. That is an existential threat.' He added:

> Yes, jihadists pose a massive threat to our security but, until the jihadists can defeat us on the battlefield they cannot destroy our nation. The Russians are different – and this is the truly terrifying bit – as they appear to be prepared to use nuclear weapons, based on recent, very public comments by Vladimir Putin.

Shirreff's novel had a very senior military crony of the Russian President toadying up to the Boss:

> That is the true genius of your plan, Vladimir Vladimirovich. NATO and the West will think this is about Russian speakers, but it is also about the balance of power in Europe. When NATO fails to react to our seizure of the Baltic states it will have failed, been defeated, and probably collapse. At that moment it will cease to pose a threat to Russia. Without NATO, Europe will be forced to beg us not to go any further. And apart from eastern Poland, which historically

has been part of Russia, we probably won't. We'll be happy to visit Paris as a tourist.

Spoiler alert: if you want to read the novel, skip this paragraph. Although Russian forces take the Baltics easily, resistance is continued in the forests. Western special forces manage to penetrate the Russian enclave of Kaliningrad to turn the nuclear-armed missiles against Moscow, after a very clever cyber-attack. The Russians withdraw from the Baltics, and Putin is mysteriously, and conveniently, 'accidentalized' in a helicopter crash.

In real life some of General Shirreff's warnings were heeded. NATO decided to send four battalions of troops to the Baltics, including one from Britain. A handful of front-line aircraft, such as the Typhoons, were also sent. Ironically, these were originally designed at the height of Cold War Mark 1 to outclass Russian fighters. Then everybody assumed that that role would be redundant. America also appeared to be beefing up its armoured reinforcement and more troops were sent to Poland and Romania.

NATO was beginning to reinforce its conventional capability to avoid the rapid resort to 'tactical' nuclear weapons. To the West, Putin became Vlad the Invader, but to even his critics at home he was Ivan the Bearable. It is the first time since Hitler that European borders had been changed by force. Putin was dangerous but he was not apparently mad. Would the invasion of eastern Ukraine be his last territorial demand?

Chapter Eight

The Russian Invasion of Ukraine

On 24 February 2022 the Russians launched a full-scale invasion of Ukraine: this was a massive escalation of the low-level war that had been festering since 2014 in eastern Ukraine and the Crimea. For months beforehand, Russia had been holding major 'exercises', while the Kremlin was also demanding legal prohibitions to stop Ukraine joining NATO.

American intelligence had been warning Kyiv for some months that the 100,000 Russian troops would probably attack but the Ukrainian government dismissed the threat. British military intelligence also took the threat seriously, although some in the British government publicly dismissed it all as bullying and bluff.

The CIA and MI6 broke many rules before and after the invasion by releasing classified intelligence, partly to prevent Russian false-flag operations. The material was chosen very carefully so as not to damage future operations. The agencies also warned the UN that Russian military commanders had lists of Ukrainians who were to be killed or sent to camps following the planned military occupation.

In December 2021 the US president warned Putin that America would take 'strong economic and other measures' if he chose to attack his neighbour. In January 2022 Russian forces moved troops into Belarus for joint 'military exercises. Washington started to provide millions of dollars of security aid to Kyiv. On 24 January 2022 NATO forces, especially in the east, were put on standby. There had been no major war in Europe since the end of the Second World War. Could the unimaginable happen and could tanks once more roll over the rich black soil of Ukraine's fertile wheatfields? Would Russian tanks fight German Panzers returned to the Ukraine battlefields in a replay, and awful déjà vu, of the massive Kursk tank battles of July-August 1943? Most military experts were incapable of conceiving of such a historical replay.

A partial answer came with the escalation of fighting in the two separatist republics in eastern Ukraine. Moscow recognized the two statelets, the Donetsk People's Republic and the Luhansk People's Republic, and sent in regular Russian forces. Sanctions were imposed by most NATO countries.

Just before the war started, the UK Ministry of Defence were using a code before secure communications were set up with Kyiv. Ben Wallace, the UK Secretary of State for Defence, had been in the Scottish parliament and had formerly served with the Scots Guards, so he decided to choose whiskies as code for weapons. NLAWS were Glenfiddich and Harpoon anti-ship missiles were Islay, for example. No one knows if the Russians were fooled.

Two days before the war started, Putin held a meeting of his National Security Council. Normally it had been a very secretive body. This time it was televised in the immense, domed circular blue and white Catherine Hall of the Kremlin.

> Putin was shown sitting at a desk at one side, interrogating his top officials, ranged before him in a semi-circle, twenty yards away. One by one, they assured him of their support, like frightened boyars pledging allegiance. It was the *mise-en-scène* of a monarch, a display of raw power, designed to show that the leadership was united but in reality making clear that all the decisions were taken by one man. The liberal newspaper *Novaya Gazeta* reported afterwards that the most powerful men in Russia had been shown like zombies, with gloomy, tense faces ... afraid to look at each at each other, paralysed with fear.[1]

The start of the invasion

Putin announced his 'special military operation'. Rockets rained down on key Ukrainian cities, while Russian fighter jets swarmed in to establish air superiority. Or at least to try to. Russian forces landed in Mariupol and troops poured in from Senkivka where Ukrainian territory meets Russia and Belarus while regular troops entered Ukraine from Crimea; the pro-Russian militias and regulars also moved out from Donetsk. Western intelligence sources thought the Russians would quickly envelop the capital and knock out the Ukrainian government by a swift decapitation strategy.

Western intelligence was right that the 'heavy metal diplomacy' was not a bluff. The reaction in President Zelensky's office was shock, not fear. The Speaker of the Ukrainian parliament, Ruslan Stefanchuk, met Zelensky on the first day of the war. 'It was a question of how could this be?' Stefanchuk added, 'We sensed the world order collapsing.'[2]

Washington offered President Zelensky a bolthole; instead, the leader ensured the safety of his family in Ukraine, stayed in Kyiv and then declared martial law. This was going to be a real fight, although most Western experts predicted a short war.

The decapitation strategy failed because of the surprisingly better trained and determined Ukrainian forces. NATO trainers and most, though not all, British and American special forces left quickly, although key trainers decamped just across the Polish border.

An important initial battle took place at Hostomel Airport, a suburb of Kyiv. Russian paratroopers arrived by helicopter early in the morning. The Rapid Response Brigade of the Ukrainian National Guard fought hard to retake the airport, shooting down three of the over thirty Russian choppers in the fight. The failure to capture and hold this airport swiftly was one of the main reasons why the decapitation strategy failed and, of course, the Kremlin expected Zelensky to take up Joe Biden's personal offer of a safe haven. Zelensky also urged Kyiv residents to start building up stockpiles of Molotov cocktails while distributing 18,000 rifles to volunteers with some military experience or training.

Troops flowed out of the two rebel republics and the Russia also swiftly took Kherson and thus control of the North Crimean Canal and so Russians turned on the tap for water to the parched peninsula. Fighting even took place in the ghost city of Chernobyl as the entombed nuclear plant came under Russian control. Snake Island fell in the south after the border guards there literally told a Russian warship to отвал (fuck off). Their refusal to surrender to an overwhelmingly powerful naval opponent led to their bravado going viral on social media. Zelensky said that 137 Ukrainians, civilian and military, had been killed on the first day of the invasion. Kyiv ordered a general mobilization of males between 18 and 60 years old; they were also banned from leaving the country.

Colonel General Oleksandr Syrsky, 57, took command of Ukrainian ground forces. A bookish figure compared with the burly medallioned Russian generals, he was born in Russia and had trained at the Russian equivalent of Sandhurst. He had fought in Afghanistan and led well in the fighting in the Donbas. He proved to be an inspiring leader, especially in the defence of Kyiv and the recapture of Kharkiv.

The Ukrainians were fighting back hard and the invading columns attempting to encircle Kyiv were being ambushed by anti-tank weapons fired by small groups of Ukrainian fighters. Right from the start of the 'war' – only Russia called it a 'special military operation' – the Ukrainians lambasted the Kremlin for deliberately targeting civilian infrastructure such as railway stations, shopping centres and also hospitals. Meanwhile, the Pentagon warned Kyiv that the Russians had actually deployed only 30 per cent of the 150,000–180,000 troops it had first amassed.

Initial talks about a peace deal were in currency when Zelensky said he was not afraid to talk about a neutral status and Putin said to Xi Jinping, the Chinese leader, that Russia was prepared to talk at high level with Ukraine. Secret high-level talks were held in Belarus between the two conflicting governments. No breakthrough emerged because Russia was demanding Ukraine's neutrality, denazification and demilitarization and recognition of Crimea as part of Russia. The war, however, was to drag on and on, with no further real Russo-Ukraine peace talks.

Surrounded on three sides, Kyiv city fought on as Mayor Vitaly Klitschko imposed a curfew from 5.00 pm to 8.00 am. Stories of secret enemy sabotage and recce groups abounded; some were no doubt true. Perhaps worse for many engrossed in social media, the internet went down in parts of the country. Billionaire Elon Musk announced he had turned on the Starlink service in Ukraine with 'many more terminals' about to be made ready.

Ramzan Kadyrov, the pro-Moscow Chechen chieftain, had deployed his men into Ukraine, and one of his SF groups was said to be planning to assassinate Zelensky. Regular Russian army forces meanwhile killed numerous citizens in Bucha and Irpin suburbs north-west of Kyiv; many rapes were reported. When the Russians were pushed out of the Kyiv area the Ukrainians discovered hundreds of local corpses, some mutilated. As in most wars, however, atrocities were committed on both sides; Ukrainian forces killed some Russian troops who were trying to surrender.

Moscow committed more men to the war and satellites showed a Russian column of tanks, APCs and self-propelled artillery crawling along the northern road to Kyiv. Initially, the column was said to be seventeen miles long but some experts suggested it was at least twice as long. Ukrainian forces picked off many of the vehicles, some of which had run out of fuel. The Ukrainians used their Bayraktar drones and small teams deployed their powerful Javelin and NLAW anti-tank missiles supplied by the USA and Britain. The disorganized Russians were outfought but, above all, out-thought.

In the south the Russians captured Melitopol amid fierce fighting, some hand-to-hand in the tight urban environment, and then war moved on to Mariupol, while some of the bitter-enders went underground in the main steel works and fought on for months. In the north, however, President Lukashenko said that Belarus would not enter the fray, although it was clearly assisting Russian troops in transit. Kherson fell on 2 March.

Zelensky spoke about direct talks with Putin while quietly welcoming large shipments of German weapons, especially surface-to-air missiles. The Ukrainian president also welcomed the arrival of foreign volunteers to help in the war effort. Many were genuine veteran volunteers from NATO armies. But Jens Stoltenberg, the NATO Secretary General, rejected Ukraine's request for a no-fly zone because that could quickly escalate to an air war and then a general conflict between Russia and the Western alliance.

The Zaporizhzhia nuclear plant, Europe's biggest, was hit a number of times and eventually captured by the Russians. The US said that the Kremlin had fired more than 500 missiles into Ukraine, often into civilian areas. Over 200,000 civilians were allowed to evacuate Mariupol although the temporary ceasefire there broke down and many remained trapped. A second ceasefire broke down. Meanwhile up to five million Ukrainian women and children were fleeing into neighbouring countries and others were moving as internal refugees to the relative security of western Ukraine. The UK made special arrangements to pay volunteers families to take in tens of thousands of Ukrainians, all this at a time of maximum political furore about illegal immigration to Britain.

Poland was the most gung-ho of frontline NATO states. Warsaw offered to transfer all its twenty-three MiG-29 fighters for free to the US air base in Ramstein in Germany. Poland could expect some frontline American fighters to replace them but it argued that this was a backstairs way of sending fighters to help Ukraine. Kyiv's demand for US F-16s became a daily mantra during the first year of the war, so much so that a Jewish military expert said Zelensky was just like his favourite Jewish grandmother: 'You never write, you never call, you never send me F-16s.'

Washington eventually relented in August 2023 and allowed two NATO allies, Denmark and Holland, to send around forty-two of the ageing F-16s in small batches but only once Ukrainians were fully trained to fly them.

By 15 March Russia had not secured air supremacy as the Ukrainian air force struck the occupied military air base next to the Kherson International airport and destroyed a range of Russian helicopters. The Western media were full of stories about how up to 40,000 Syrian fighters were offering to join the Russian side but little actual evidence of that emerged over the following months.

The Ukrainians had started to push back the Russian ground forces, not least around Kyiv, but the long-distance missile attacks continued, including targets in the far west, in Lviv where fuel depots were hit. On 16 March the Regional Drama Theatre in Mariupol was bombed; it was sheltering around 1,000 civilians. Aerial photographs showed the word 'civilians' in Russian in big letters and spelled out why the Russians should not attack. The number of actual fatalities was never clearly established. The Russians were winding down their unsuccessful decapitation encirclement of Kyiv, taking massive casualties amid the destruction of large number of tanks and APCs. The focus of the assault began to switch to the Donbas. Ukrainian military intelligence said Putin was now trying to split Ukraine in a 'Korean scenario'.

By late March Mariupol had been bombed to 'dust' as Kyiv described it, while the invading forces were evacuating tens of thousands of civilians, especially children, to Russia for resettlement, often against their will.

At the end of March Russian and Ukrainian negotiators met in Istanbul under the aegis of the Turkish president who said that the Kyiv government was prepared to renounce any plans for NATO membership and to make Russian a second official language in Ukraine. Recognition of Russian control of Crimea and removal of all Russian forces to pre-invasion positions could be discussed later. Putin blamed Kyiv for the breakdown of the talks partly because it refused to introduce laws to curb neo-Nazism in the country.

Ukraine denied any involvement in a series of explosions in the Russian city of Belgorod just across the border. A Russian military camp was hit by shells from the Ukrainian side, killing at least four people, according to the Kremlin. Ukraine's NATO backers grew increasingly concerned about the territorial spread of the fighting, especially if NATO-supplied long-range weapons were to be used against Russian territory. The Russians later said that two Ukrainian Mi-24 military helicopters had struck a fuel storage depot in Belgorod.

The failure of the decapitation offensive against Kyiv became obvious when the Russian army withdrew all the way to Chernobyl, leaving the Ukrainians in charge of all the Kyiv Oblast (district). Soon a number of massacres were literally unearthed. According to Bucha's mayor, 280 bodies were hastily buried in mass graves. Human Rights Watch, and Western media, reported on, and produced evidence of, war crimes in the occupied areas of Ukraine: executions, rapes, torture and looting. Zelensky accused Russia of genocide and said that Western sanctions were not enough to punish the invader. He also asked for anti-aircraft systems, artillery, armoured vehicles and, especially, ammunition. The Ukrainians were soon expending more 155mm shells in a month than the US could produce in a year.

Kyiv was understandably anxious to get new guns – with enough ammunition. The Soviet heritage of 152mm calibre guns compared with NATO standard 155mm artillery meant that on three millimetres the fate of Europe could hang.

Western military experts disagreed constantly on this war. Most thought the Russians would swamp the Ukrainians in days, while some intelligence insiders knew the extent and quality of NATO training and new weapons supplies. As the war dragged on, some external experts argued that Ukraine should trade territory for peace while others thought that the obvious Russian incompetence in the first weeks and months, plus lots of NATO aid, could contain the Russian army and might even allow a Ukrainian victory, provided Moscow did not resort to tactical nukes.

It soon became an artillery war with Ukraine being vastly outgunned and outnumbered by the Russians who had always been believers in the dictum that 'artillery is the god of war'. The Americans soon contributed massive amounts of artillery weapons and ammunition, running down their own stocks so that in the end they had to deploy the much-criticized cluster munitions.

In the North the Ukrainians had more than held their ground but in the north-east there was hard fighting in and around Sumy. In the south the Russians took control of the giant Zaporizhzhia nuclear plant. Despite some damage to the plant, the International Atomic Energy Agency (IAEA) explained it was not leaking any radiation. A meltdown at this plant could have dwarfed the Chernobyl catastrophe. On 2 March Kherson fell, the first major Ukrainian city to be captured. Mariupol fell except for the Azovstal steel mill where the Ukrainians fought on desperately and without much hope of relief. On 30 April 2022 civilians sheltering in the Azovstal complex were allowed to leave under UN protection. Over 2,000 Ukrainian troops remained, still fighting although hundreds were wounded. Zelensky had ordered them to surrender but the deputy commander of the besieged troops, Illia Somoilenko, said 'We are basically dead men. Most of us know this and that's why we fight so fearlessly.' While Putin promised proper PoW treatment some prominent Russian lawmakers called on the Russian government to deny prisoner exchange for the Ukrainian survivors, many from the tough Azov Regiment that the Kremlin described as a Nazi organization.

Although missile attacks continued, not least on urban centres throughout the country, the Russian advance slowed down and another unnamed US defence official in Washington called the Russian advance 'very tepid' and 'anaemic'. Well, he could say that as no one was firing missiles at Washington. But anaemic or not, Russia was taking heavy casualties and started recruiting volunteer battalions from the regions and later from the prisons.

The Russians kept attacking Odesa with missiles and artillery. The Kremlin hinted that they could occupy the whole coastline to include their protected statelet of Transnistria; Ukraine then would be a landlocked state with no access to the Black Sea. Meanwhile Ukrainian forces apparently blew up two transmitters in Transnistria that were broadcasting Russian television programmes. On 30 June the Russians announced they had withdrawn from Snake Island, 120 miles from Odesa, because of Ukrainian military pressure. Odesa was the last major port for Ukraine to export grain in a UN and Turkish-brokered deal to secure a sea corridor for grain and other foodstuffs, especially to relieve the famine conditions in North Africa.

French President Macron, one of the few NATO leaders still in regular communication with Putin, arranged for a local ceasefire around the Zaporizhzhia nuclear plant because the Ukraine government claimed that the Russians had placed missile launchers and heavy artillery between the separate reactor walls of the main nuclear installation as a shield against Ukrainian counter-attack. Putin allowed IAEA inspectors to visit the plant. Some experts on NATO argued that any deliberate damage to the plant causing radiation leaks would contaminate Alliance members, and therefore would lead to an activation of Article 5 of the NATO treaty.

Ukrainian counter-offensives

On 6 September 2022, the Ukrainians launched a surprise counter-offensive in the Kharkiv area. The Russians fell back, further denting the image of invincible Russian forces. On 21 September Putin announced a partial mobilization. And in an act of bravado Putin announced the annexation of the regions of Donetsk, Luhansk, Kherson and Zaporizhzhia even though not all parts of the oblasts were controlled by Russian forces. Ukraine, the UN, the USA and EU all denounced the annexations as illegal.

The Russian positions in the north-east of Ukraine collapsed as the invaders retreated to Izium. According to the UK Ministry of Defence intelligence briefings, the Russians had also abandoned 'various high-value military assets'.

In October the Ukrainians moved successfully on Kherson while the Russians withdrew in good order to the eastern bank of the Dnieper. Kherson was retaken.

Winter war

After the success of the twin offensives capturing Kharkiv and Kherson, the front line froze into a winter stalemate. The Russians did try to launch a winter offensive but if it failed because of lack of trained men and supply problems, especially with artillery ammunition. In February the Kremlin mobilized nearly 200,000 fresh, if often inexperienced, troops to fight in the Donbas, while Ukrainians troops were worn out by a year of heavy fighting. The Kremlin introduced the Wagner Group especially to take part in the 'grinding advances' around the city of Bakhmut. Tens of thousands of troops from the prison battalions also took part in suicidal frontal assaults around Bakhmut.

Elsewhere, around the coal-mining town of Vuhledar, in late January the largest armoured battle of the war led the UK Ministry of Defence to report that the Russians had lost at least 130 tanks and APCs.

After the defeats at Kharkiv and Kherson, the Russians were determined to proclaim victory somewhere – somehow. Despite its lack of strategic importance, Bakhmut became the iconic symbol of Russian re-assertion. At great cost, the Russian army took the nearby salt-mine city of Soledar. Eventually the encirclement of nearby Bakhmut followed with the Ukrainians hanging on to small eastern bits of the city. By 26 March 2023 the Wagner Group had claimed to control the whole of Bakhmut, though perhaps only 5 per cent of the city remained in Ukrainian hands. In May some small areas of the territory around Bakhmut were re-captured by the Ukrainians.

The summer counter-offensive (June-August 2023)

Over nearly a year, the Russians had erected a very coherent and interlocking set of defensive systems – ditches, trenches, barbed wire, dragon's teeth to stop armoured vehicles; three layers of defensive fortifications lay along the nearly 800 miles of the front line. All were mutually supported and were constructed with a professional rigour not readily shown so far in the fighting.

The Ukrainians took back a few settlements and continued to probe, but not committing the bulk of their new NATO armour and Western-trained troops. They were probing, looking for a weakness in the defensive walls. The counter-offensive appeared to stall for months as Kyiv worried about committing its new weapons, especially without any air supremacy. The Russians were playing a waiting game, assuming that their defences would hold even when the Ukrainians deployed cluster weapons that are ideal for offensives against entrenched troops.

Recapturing a city – say Bakhmut – would be pointless if it bled Ukraine dry. What mattered was degrading the Russian will to fight. Perhaps as many 100,000 Ukrainians, twenty brigades, with nine of them with new NATO armour, were involved, although most of the Ukrainian troops were in reserve waiting for the breakthrough. The Russians had about 200,000 men; some of the newly mobilized reservists of questionable training and morale but they were propped up by battle-hardened professionals and veterans of the long fight. They were bunkered down in their trenches – and so far less likely to retreat in a panic even if the Ukrainians broke through. The Russians were lobbing around 10,000 artillery shells a day.

A long stalemate would play into the Kremlin's game of waiting for the West to give up. Unless Kyiv could produce some kind of win then frustration and compassion fatigue would set in among the NATO alliance members.

Chapter Nine

The Wagner Mutiny

The Ukrainians were struggling to make their counter-offensive work when suddenly Heaven bestowed a splendid gift. On 23 June 2023 the Wagner Group headed by an ever-cursing motor-mouth called Yevgeny Prigozhin, staged a rebellion against the Russian Ministry of Defence.

Prigozhin was certainly a larger-than-life character. He had done time, almost a decade in prison, before emerging as a prominent figure in the St Petersburg business community. He became famous for a string of restaurants that won the favour of Putin. Dubbed 'Putin's Chef' he became a close and trusted confidant of the Big Boss because Prigozhin fitted in perfectly with the mafia style of Russian leadership.

Prigozhin fully understood the system and made billions from it. He had been in prison and he knew that the court system, when it came to politics, was an arm of the Kremlin. The same went for parliament or elections and even the status of the oligarchs. The ex-spooks ran the show. It was a phantom system with phantom rights both for individuals and businesses. There were the occasional honest bureaucrats. A female judge who tried to play it straight went over to the dark side. As a tycoon said about her: 'It's as if she had drunk blood, she is now totally part of the system.' Anyone who crossed the Kremlin could be jailed at any time on rigged or trumped-up charges. Property rights were conditional on fealty to the Boss, Putin, whom US Senator John McCain called a 'thug, a murderer and a killer'. The one person who knew all this in more detail than anyone else was Putin's most loyal sidekick – Prigozhin, who also saw regularly the *capo mafioso* sneer when Putin was despatching an enemy. It is hard, therefore, to understand why Prigozhin decided to cross his master and mentor.

Private military companies proliferate in the US and Europe but they were and are technically illegal in Russia, although a number of private militias existed, notably to protect large mining and oil and gas companies. Putin later admitted to funding Wagner with millions of roubles from the state treasury. Wagner was formally inaugurated in early 2014 during the annexation of territory in Eastern Ukraine and Crimea. Wagner's combat reputation grew enormously during the long battle for Bakhmut in 2022–23. The Wagner mercenaries were also very active in Syria supporting the Bashar al-Assad regime. Without Russian backing in general, and Wagner in particular, the Syrian government would have been toppled. Some Russians made millions from finding ways of exploiting the Syrian dependency. Many senior officers, especially, made serious contributions to their small government pensions. Wagner was also active in Mali, Libya and the Central African Republic. Secretly, the group was also busy in Sudan mainly supporting and training the Rapid Support Forces that ended up fighting a civil war with the army.[1] Wagner was also involved in lucrative gold deals, mainly in Darfur. The Russian mercenaries earned a well-founded reputation for brutality in African conflicts but they provided a useful source of private revenue for the Kremlin. This grew more important after sanctions were imposed on Russia following the invasion of Ukraine.

Wagner's involvement in the heavy fighting in Ukraine after 2022 allowed the Kremlin to hide the unofficial casualty rates, as well as permit direct recruitment from the prisons on a six months' deal. Fight hard, become a hero and if you survive you get a pardon and a lump sum. But they were used as cannon fodder and around half died en route to posthumous hero status. A few were shot to discourage desertion.

In short, Wagner was a combat-savvy and lucrative tool of Putin's secret foreign policy. And its boss, Prigozhin, was completely trusted by Putin. After all, he was entirely Vladimir's creature and an integral part of Putin's mafia capitalism.

The problem was: the Wagner chieftain got too big for his boots, especially when he won acclaim on Russian social media for his outspoken right-wing views. Prigozhin's disputes with the top brass in the Ministry of Defence predated the invasion of Ukraine, however. There had been issues with Prigozhin's vastly profitable contracts to feed the military. During the Russo-Ukrainian war the Russians suffered heavy casualties but Putin was reluctant to announce the mobilization of reservists. So the obvious answer was to boost the Wagner Group: it was even given heavy armour and aviation assets. By late 2022 Wagner had burgeoned to perhaps as many as 50,000 fighters from around 5,000 five years before. Part of the reason was Prigozhin's permission and ability to recruit from the prisons. As a former convict he knew exactly how to appeal to the Russian inmates; his recruitment talks in the jails were widely viewed on social media, as well as his foul-mouthed tirades against the top brass, especially Defence Minister Shoigu and the head of the army, General Valery Gerasimov. The rank and file plus some officers applauded the criticism, especially of the stolid leadership at the front, poor equipment, lack of food and all the many things soldiers always grumble about. And the Russian recruits really had serious grievances about the corrupt and often inhumane system, especially the hazing of raw soldiers. So Prigozhin morphed into their national avenger and, after years of secrecy, became an international figure as his broadcasts from the front wearing combat gear were front-line news on Western TV and in Russia. His men and even some senior officers liked the way he 'got down and dirty' with his troops in the front line. Prigozhin did not criticize Putin himself but his descriptions of the ramshackle conduct of the big war – he used the term 'war' not 'special military operation' – undermined much of the official Kremlin propaganda.

In the end, in one famous broadcast surrounded by a pile of bodies of his men, he accused the army leadership of firing on the Wagner soldiers – after they had 'won' the long battle for Bakhmut. Exasperated, the military establishment insisted on clipping Wagner's wings, starting with a ban on prison recruitment. The army, still short of manpower, did revert partly to the old Soviet model of penal battalions. In 1942 they were created by Stalin – under the motto 'not one step back' after the swift Wehrmacht advances of 1941. Stalin created nearly half a million troops in the penal battalions (*Strafbats*) and few survived the war.[2] The

2023 introduction of modern Russian punishment battalions were called *Storm-Z* and they were not on the Second World War scale or survival rates. The Russians used recalcitrant existing solders, as well as, in late 2022, hoovering up young men from the prisons. The new soldiers were given up to fifteen days' training and were attached to regular army formations who were suffering from battle fatigue. The Russians tended not to rotate regularly their front-line troops for R and R.

Many in the West and Moscow were amazed at how Prigozhin's expletive-laced tirades were allowed to continue unpunished. When the Kharkiv counter-offensive was so successful, the Wagner boss went on about the Russian military command, saying, 'All these bastards ought to be sent to the front barefoot with just a machine gun.' He did not stop with the military leadership, he also had a go at parliamentarians and especially the elite who were sending their sons abroad while ordinary Russians were fighting and dying for their country in Ukraine. What the Wagner boss actually said (in a polite translation) was: 'We won't allow Shoigu's daughters and sons-in-law to sit and lubricate their asses with Vaseline while grandmothers and children die like dogs in Belgorod [near Ukraine border] … And it's not so far from Belgorod to Rublevka [a prestigious and very upmarket suburb in Western Moscow].'

Even more pointedly, Prigozhin claimed that the two places in Russia that NATO would never attack were the headquarters of the General Staff in Moscow and the army's command post in Rostov-on-Don because, if the enemy did succeed in taking out Russia's army command, 'We might have a chance of winning this war.'

Prigozhin even went as far as comparing the differences in society in 2023 with those existing before the 1917 revolution. But the crescendo of his verbal onslaught was during the final stages of the Bakhmut battle. Sergei Shoigu and the Chief of the General Staff, Valery Gerasimov, were singled out as responsible for the deaths of many thousands of Wagner fighters because of the inadequate ammunition supplies. When the Wagner Group claimed victory in Bakhmut the mercenaries handed the city over to regular forces but, on 3 and 5 June 2023, Prigozhin claimed that they were attacked by the army and that mines were laid on the route of their withdrawal from Bakhmut. Then Prigozhin complained that his highly lucrative and long-term catering contracts for the military were being stopped.

The march on Rome

In mid-June Wagner troops were ordered to sign formal contacts with the army. The final prize for their bloody Bakhmut efforts was absorption into the regulars. All special forces, even hardened jailbirds, anywhere in the world, would have baulked at that kind of deal. Prigozhin's private army was going to be taken from him and also his lucrative sidelines in Africa and the Middle East. He hinted that his opponents in the army high command should be executed and that a potential uprising against the incompetent officials could happen.

Western intelligence gathered data on Wagner preparing equipment, ammunition and vehicles near the Russian border and they worked out that a rebellion was about to happen but, apparently, they did not know the date. Their communication intercepts and satellite intelligence continued to build a picture of Wagner fighting back against the Russian ministry of defence order to integrate the mercenaries into the regular army.

The Wagner boss claimed that his decision to invade his own country was made at the last minute in a moment of anger. Western intelligence suggested that the plot had been hatched over some time. The powerful General Sergey Surovikin, nicknamed 'General Armageddon' during his ruthless suppression of opponents in Syria, apparently had knowledge of the planned insurrection. He was hardly a radical. As a veteran of the Soviet–Afghan War, the civil war in Tajikistan, and Second Chechen War, as well as his service in the Levant, he was not one of nature's rebels. He was very close to Prigozhin and was said to hold a VIP membership card of the Wagner Group. Perhaps as many as thirty other high-ranking military and intelligence officials were in on the conspiracy. Strangely, the FSB was not aware until a short time before the coup was supposed to take off. Or maybe they were aware but not telling the president.

The original plan was to arrest the two men Prigozhin hated most, Shoigu and Gerasimov, when they were due to visit Rostov-on-Don, the main army supply base for the Ukraine war. The FSB tipped them off but were still reluctant to inform the president. The general suspicion was that Prigozhin was bluffing. They didn't realize how serious and widespread the conspiracy was until Rostov fell without any opposition. To the contrary, the Wagner Group soldiers were welcomed by many military people and nobody offered any armed resistance.

In a video released on 23 June 2023 Prigozhin shredded the Kremlin's argument for the war. Ukraine had not acted in any way aggressively before the invasion. He maintained that some of the military leadership had personal motives for initiating a war and that they were hiding the number of casualties, even when up to a thousand soldiers were killed each day. Prigozhin, perhaps as a pretext for rebellion, claimed on 23 June, on Telegram channels that the Russian Ministry of Defence had killed over 2,000 of his fighters with missile attacks on their rear bases. Western authorities interpreted the pictures as fakes.

Many of Prigozhin's men were unprepared for a military rebellion as they started to mobilize for a series of convoys aimed at Moscow. General Surovikin called on Wagner to stop but some media experts described his appeal as a 'hostage-style' video. Thereafter he disappeared. The army and the National Guard deployed armoured vehicles around Moscow especially on the M4 highway from Rostov-on-Don, which the Wagner troops had seized in the early morning of 24 June.

Sporting silver armbands, the Wagner men took control of the Southern Military District HQ and set up roadblocks in the streets around the perimeter. Video of Prigozhin arguing with the Deputy Defence Minister and Deputy Chief of Staff was aired widely. The Wagner boss was telling the senior officers to bring Shoigu and Gerasimov to a meeting with him. The local authorities told residents to stay at home. Many locals did come onto the streets and warmly greeted the Wagner men who were on their very best behaviour. Some Rostov residents did argue with them, however. Chechen paramilitaries were said to be in the vicinity and prepared to take on the Wagner mercenaries but no engagements were reported.

On the morning of 24 June, two convoys, one from Rostov and one directly from occupied Ukrainian territory moved towards Moscow. They consisted of a few thousand men with tanks on transporters and anti-aircraft weapons, armoured cars and some civilian vehicles. Prigozhin claimed 25,000 of his men were involved, though Moscow and Western intelligence put it at less than 8,000 and perhaps half of those were in the lead convoy.

Halfway to Moscow, at Voronzeh, the convoy was attacked by the Russian Air Force. Two helicopters were shot down, including a command helicopter. British sources estimated the number of air force personnel killed as high as twenty-nine. There was some fighting in the city and TV showed pictures of a fuel depot being blown up.

Wagner troops moved on to the Lipetsk Oblast, about 250 miles south of Moscow; in that oblast authorities had deliberately demolished parts of the highway using excavators, and by deploying buses and trucks to block the roads. The army set up defensive lines along the Oka river that flows south of the Russian capital. The mayor of Moscow introduced a counter-terrorism regime; rumours abounded that airline tickets had sold out, partly because Putin was alleged to have fled to St Petersburg, his original power base. In truth the president probably remained in the Kremlin. Posters advertising Wagner recruitment were quickly torn down and the FSB raided the Wagner HQ in St Petersburg and said they had seized millions in US dollars as well as gold bars. Prigozhin in turn claimed that the money was partly for compensation for fallen comrades and the US currency was used for covert operations in Africa and the USA. In Syria the Russian military and Syrian intelligence quickly clamped down on Wagner and cut their communications with Russia. They were then offered regular army contracts that were difficult to refuse, despite the pay cuts.

Prigozhin tried to speak to Putin but the president refused to take his calls. Eventually President Alexander Lukashenko was asked to intervene. Despite Putin's bloodcurdling threats on a special TV announcement, Prigozhin promised to return to the southern bases in exchange for security guarantees for his men. The Wagner chieftain explained that he had not planned a coup and was standing down to avoid bloodshed with fellow Russians. The Wagner men mostly returned to their bases in occupied Ukraine but some moved to Belarus.

The Kremlin announced that Wagner fighters would not face prosecution and they had the choice of joining the regular army or going into exile in Belarus with their leader. This was a major climbdown for the president, whose control looked very shaky for some time. On 24 June Putin's TV address had denounced the Wagner Group's actions as 'treason' and said Russia's very existence was under threat, just as in 1917. Some overseas opponents of Putin, such as the former oil magnate, Mikhail Khodorkovsky, urged Russians 'to support even the devil' if he decided to take on the Kremlin. The Russian public remained largely passive although many ordinary citizens in Rostov-on-Don welcomed the rebels.

In the West most leaders said little, partly because they did not want to give the Kremlin any excuse to portray the domestic rebellion as a foreign conspiracy. The Kyiv government was far more vocal saying that the plot demonstrated how unstable Russia was, although there was little evidence of how the debacle had impacted the battlefield.

On 26 June Prigozhin again defended the insurrection insisting that he did not want to lead a coup against the government. Cheekily, he favourably compared Wagner's actions to credibly threaten to capture Moscow with the Russian army's failure to take Kyiv.

The FSB said it stopped investigating the Wagner coup and closed the books, while a BBC investigation in late June rang a large number of recruitment centres with local Russian phones and confirmed that they were all still signing contracts with the Wagner Group.

Prigozhin's business empire was wound down, especially Wagner's propaganda machine and trolling farms. And Wagner was forced to hand over all the tanks and missile systems to the army. And yet the US Department of Defense claimed that Wagner was heavily back into the Ukrainian fighting. The Russian defence ministry video also showed Wagner instructing Belarus army troops near the capital Minsk. Kyiv said that Wagner had hundreds of men there who could destabilize the northern border.

Putin did initiate a major purge of his security and intelligence elites. At least fifteen of the top brass were variously said to be 'resting', under interrogation, or in prison. General Sergey Surovikin appeared to have been arrested, for example. Some right-wing pro-Russian extremists in the two Donbas republics were also detained.

Prigozhin appeared to be a dead man walking but he re-appeared in St Petersburg and he met with Putin alongside other senior Wagner commanders. Prigozhin said he would no longer fight in Ukraine but instead train soldiers in Belarus and maintain the African operations. And Prigozhin was seen smiling and meeting African leaders at the African-Russia summit in St Petersburg in late July.

Had Putin and the Wagner boss really kissed and made up? Some experts suggested that a lot of what had happened had been a con to show that any alternative to Putin would come from the loony right. Unlikely. Some cynics even suggested that the whole episode had been a charade to flush out disloyal elements in the regime, especially in the military and intelligence agencies. Putin looked more vulnerable than at any time in his twenty-three-year rule. The president had always been an icon of stability and yet a relatively small number of soldiers had almost marched on Moscow and may have taken the Kremlin. Maybe. That Putin had apparently forgiven the alleged traitors made him look weak. Many Western experts on Russia started to talk about the beginning of the end for Putin's reign.

In mid-August 2023, the UK Ministry of Defence reported that the Kremlin had decided to defund Wagner. Putin had lied about the funding before, so the truth was hard to decipher. Wagner had been very useful to Putin although his desire to clip its wings after the mutiny was obvious. He wanted the foreign income without any political challenge and with the deniability, such an important issue to a veteran spook. The partial move of Wagner to Belarus might have indicated that that the allied state might fund the group (unofficially, since militias were still illegal in Russia, the Kremlin could provide cash). Wagner had proved to be a potent fighting force in Africa and the Middle East as well as in Ukraine so it would be kept on even if some of its battle-hardened soldiers had joined the regular army. The military leadership of the group would need refreshing, however. It could go full-circle and repeat the original formation. The first military commander was a GRU special forces lieutenant colonel called Dimitry Utkin. Utkin's original call-sign was Wagner, to show his appreciation of Hitler's favourite composer. At 53, he could take Prigozhin's place despite his (very) colourful past.

It was not to be.

On 23 August 2023 a small private jet carrying Prigozhin and Utkin was apparently brought down by surface-to-air missiles near Moscow. Others conjectured it was a bomb planted on board, in a crate of wine, it was said. The Kremlin furiously denied any involvement – but they would do that, wouldn't they? Probably Putin didn't mind that nearly the whole of Russia assumed he had taken his revenge. You don't mess with the Boss.

And yet it still might all backfire. If Putin had so much trouble controlling one of his very own creatures, what did that make of his so-called iron hand? He had also changed his mind and certainly gone back on his word. Many in the top elites knew that the system worked on nods and winks. It made them very uneasy. It was (likely) the work of the FSB and the first 'spectacular' on home soil.

Putin sent condolences to Prigozhin's family, whom he knew well from years of close ties in St Petersburg. The deaths of the Wagner boss and his Number Two, Utkin, were also confirmed after DNA testing – removing perhaps one conspiracy theory that the Wagner chieftains had switched planes at the last minute.

The US armed forces used mercenaries, really ex-military private contractors, extensively in Iraq and Afghanistan but they were very much subordinate to the Pentagon. And it could be argued that the British use of Nepal's tough volunteers (around 3,000 still in service) was a form of mercenary recruitment.

In a powerful essay in the UK *Daily Mail* on 26 August, Boris Johnson – of course a big fan of President Zelensky and who said that Putin had threatened to kill him – asked the obvious question: why did Prigozhin believe Putin?, whom he knew to be a killer, especially of those whom he thought had betrayed him – the poison killings in London and Salisbury were obvious examples. Most experts in the intelligence game assumed that Prigozhin's only real chance was to have gone all the way to take the Kremlin. Thereafter, he was 'a dead man walking' to use the cliched term, if he stayed in Russia or Belarus. He might have survived longer if he had hidden himself away in somewhere lawless such as Darfur though not a great place for a man who liked fine wines. And even then he would have spent the rest of his shortish life, without his family, forever looking over his shoulder, assuming that whatever side won the Sudanese civil war would let him stay on.

Former Prime Minster Johnson wrote:

> As we watch the chilling footage of that plane spiralling to earth, we are witnessing something historic. This the violent liquidation – on TV – of his enemies by an existing head of state. I cannot think of another example of such ostentation and uninhibited savagery by a world leader – not in our lifetimes.

Boris Johnson continued his righteous tirade by comparing Putin's televised tribute to the dead Wagnerites as from the pages of the *Godfather*. 'Putin wanted to kill Prigozhin with maximum global éclat and at a time of his own choosing.'

Even Alexei Navalny entered the fray. From prison he said that the assassination of Prigozhin would make him a martyr to his followers and it could 'plunge Russia into a savage civil war'.

The key question is whether Putin's cronies see this as an act of strength or weakness.

Chapter Ten

The Role of Sanctions

The popular mood in the West became very anti-Russian. Even Russian-themed restaurants were targeted and the provincial government in Ontario encouraged local shops to ban all Russian goods, even vodka. Many innocent Russians from professors to musicians working in the West were denounced if they did not publicly disown Putin's actions. The day after the invasion the Russian tennis player Andrey Rubley, after playing in the Dubai tournament, did the usual trick of writing on a camera lens: his message was 'No war please'. Sports people were specially hit hard and FIFA suspended the Russian national team from the World Cup. Sometimes, the anti-Russian feeling was no doubt due to genuine moral revulsion at the atrocities committed in the invasion. At other times it seemed more to do with virtue signalling. The Cardiff Philharmonic Orchestra cancelled a concert of music by Tchaikovsky. The great Russian master died in 1893, a little before Putin invaded. But organizers said that the use of cannon fire in the *1812 Overture*, although reminding music lovers of Napoleon's defeat, was too reminiscent of cannon fire in 2022. Then Netflix stopped their production of *Anne Karenina*. No writer captures warfare in Russia more powerfully than Leo Tolstoy, a former soldier turned Russia's most famous pacifist in the last three decades of his life.

But these were more gesture and cultural politics. What hit much harder were the approximately 6,000-plus sanctions imposed by Western governments – mainly the EU, North America and NATO. The Western countries also controlled much of the banking systems, especially the SWIFT system; this cut Russia off from some global trading mechanisms. The rouble and the Russian stock market took a dive but soon recovered because some (milder) sanctions had been imposed in 2014 and Moscow had built up reserves and hoarded extra cash in Chinese banks, for example, with a relatively small amount in US dollars. Billions, however, were frozen in the West as NATO states talked of using the money to rebuild Ukraine after the war. Meanwhile, the Russian central bank enforced strict measures to stop capital flight. One of the main aspects of sanctions was Russian energy exports. Before the invasion Moscow had sent half its oil exports to Europe and so Russia had to sell more oil to China and India. The war completely shook up the energy markets and pushed up the price of oil and gas. Paradoxically, Russia was selling far less energy to Europe but making more money. Both NATO and Russia claimed to be winning the sanctions wars, though in fact both sides appeared to be suffering.

While agriculture was shattered in Ukraine, it was different in Russia. Mikhail Gorbachev used to joke that Soviet agriculture had been a disaster since 1917. Under Putin, farming was booming. In Soviet times Russia had imported food but in modern Russia food exports, not least to starving North Africa, was bringing in more money than arms sales.

After the invasion of Ukraine, however, almost a thousand independent companies such as Apple cut back or ended their involvement with Russia, partly because of reputational risks rather than any government edicts. McDonalds was one of the first to arrive in Moscow and then one of the most prominent exiteers. Russia was good at finding local substitutes for burgers and crucial electronic components but they were often of lower quality and certainly higher price. Russian airlines were especially affected as 80 per cent of the commercial airlines were supplied by Boeing and Airbus. Without spare parts and technical support, many planes were grounded. And Russian airlines were denied the right to fly in the airspace of many countries. Many individual Russians, especially wealthy cronies of Putin in business and parliament (300 in the Duma), were targeted. And Western media made propaganda headlines about seizing luxury yachts and private jets owned by the oligarchs. Joe Biden warned, 'We are coming after your ill-gotten gains.'

Most of the yachts were sailed to safe harbours in Russia or the Gulf states and much of the property assets in London and Paris was transferred to non-sanctioned owners or front companies in the Caribbean. Meanwhile ordinary Russians suffered but so did ordinary Europeans. The USA imported little Russian energy but the European leadership soon worked out that buying Russian energy was merely subsidising Moscow's invasion. Coal was easier to finesse, not least because of reducing carbon emissions anyway because of global warming. Oil was tougher as some EU countries, such as Slovakia, relied on Moscow for nearly all its supplies. Gas was more difficult than oil and more expensive to ship. Using liquefied natural gas from elsewhere required specially-built port facilities. Germany was hardest hit because it had to abandon the massive investment in the Nord Stream 2 that had laid 760 miles of undersea pipeline connecting Russia with eastern Germany. Berlin searched anxiously for alternatives in the US and the Middle East. Many environmentalists were cheered as they hoped the crisis could reduce carbon consumption but, in the short term, old coal and nuclear plants were kept going.

The greatest sufferers were the inhabitants of the poorest parts of North Africa, especially in the Horn where famine appeared almost endemic. Around 40 per cent of the world's wheat supplies came from Russia and Ukraine. Russia was an important exporter of fertilizer and Ukraine was a major supplier of sunflower seed oil as well as corn and barley. The war on land and especially at sea disrupted supplies. Sudan was war torn and it secured nearly all its wheat from Russia. As did its neighbours in Egypt, and Eritrea. Also, many crops could not be grown in the region because of the crucial shortage of fertilizer and much lower yields forced many marginal farmers to simply give up. Shoppers might grumble loudly in European supermarkets but many North Africans began to starve.

Leaders in the global south did not like the way America tried to enforce sanctions. They did not buy the democracy-versus-autocracy argument and attempts to preserve the so-called rules-based system. Powerful countries such as India remained neutral. Many in Africa such as South Africa remembered Russian support in the long anti-apartheid struggle. China did not back Russia formally but provided some support though both India and China told Moscow to avoid carefully the use of tactical nuclear weapons. Israel also refrained from taking sides despite a being a close military ally of Washington. Oddly, classic neutrals such as Singapore and Switzerland did partially support sanctions against Moscow.

At the time of writing in August 2023 the Russian economy began to show signs of real weakness. The value of the rouble had been falling steadily for months. In August 2022 a dollar could buy 60 roubles; now it bought 100. Military spending, above all, and sanctions were taking a toll. The value of Russian exports outside Europe dropped because of the price cap on its oil sales. Some European nations have weaned themselves off Mother Russia's gas. At the same time, imports into Russia from countries such as China and Turkey had mounted. But the rouble is not a popular form of payment and so hard dollar currency became scarce. True, the rouble plummeted at the start of the war – initially trading at 126 to the dollar. It did rally very quickly because of interest rate hikes and government controls on moving money abroad. And energy prices rose dramatically at the start. The central bank came under pressure to raise rates again. The ordinary citizens are tightening their belts yet again. And perhaps the urban elites had become too mollycoddled to emulate the resilience of their grandparents who endured the Great Patriotic War.

The cosmopolitan class still managed to get around sanctions; they had gone into new projects, such as smuggling parts for Mercedes cars or Italian handbags. This class may steal at home but they bank abroad. They send their children to good universities in Prague or London. Their fancy holidays have been curbed, however. Sure, they can still go to Phuket or the Gulf states but it upsets people who regard themselves as Europeans to be excluded from London and Paris.

The initial sanctions in 2014 and then the threat of far more severe restraints on trade did not deter Moscow from fighting. Nor does the very tough post-invasion sanctions blitz appear to be deterring Russia from maintaining its war. In the long history of sanctions from the days of the League of Nations to the sanctions against white-ruled states in southern Africa, they have never worked very well. But they often made the rich countries that imposed them *feel* better. It was usually the most innocent, often in Africa, who paid the price.

Can Russia survive the sanctions pressure? There are other examples for the Kremlin. Pyongyang and Tehran have been under sanctions for far longer than Russia but have remained secure and manage to be prominent regional and international players. Labels such as 'bigger and badder North Korea' and even 'Orthodox Iran' have been used by experts to describe the beleaguered Russian Federation.

Legal International intervention

The *Economist* Intelligence Unit in early 2023 suggested that world opinion divided roughly three ways. A third supported Russia, while a third was neutral and just over a third were against Russia. NATO was co-ordinating massive military aid to Ukraine and old Soviet states such as Bulgaria were able to supply abundant quantities of Soviet-style weapons plus fuel. Germany completely changed its foreign and defence policies to supply lethal weapons such as the famous Leopard tanks. For the first time the EU provided lethal arms. The biggest single donor was been the USA. On the other side Belarus has closely backed Russia and China had been rumoured to supply small arms and ammunition. Iran had been a big provider of drones.

One of the most prominent international actors has been the International Criminal Court (ICC) On 17 March 2023 the Court issued a warrant for Putin's arrest because Russia had illegally deported and transferred children from Ukraine to Russia. It was one of the only war crimes allegations that Moscow did not deny because it proudly declared it was saving orphans. This was the first time that the ICC had issued a warrant for the leader of one of the five permanent members of the UN Security Council. Previously, a sitting head of state, Omar Al-Bashir, the president of Sudan, had been issued with an arrest warrant. This did limit the Sudanese president's freedom to travel. Whether any country is prepared to arrest Putin if he attends an international conference is a moot point.

Chapter Eleven

Information Warfare and Propaganda

Probably this war has witnessed more lies, deliberate or accidental, than most previous conflicts. This is partly because of the explosion of social media. And everyone has a camera on their phone.

Moscow insisted on calling the war a 'special military operation'. And it was targeted against 'Nazis' trying to suppress Ukrainian Russian-speakers. And in the West those who had opposed the expansion of NATO were generally kept off the main TV channels. Ukraine was the biggest story on Western networks, according to amount of airtime, since the 9/11 atrocities. The flight of over five million women, children and elderly men from Ukraine, because men from 18–60 were not allowed to leave the country, provided endless human-interest stories throughout Europe for months. No refugee camps sprang up; ordinary people in Poland, Germany and the rest of Europe welcomed Ukrainians into their own homes. Britain had a special scheme where people were paid up to £350 a month by the government to house Ukrainians for six months. Within a year, passion fatigue reigned, even in the initially welcoming Britain. Many Ukrainians went back home and some became homeless in Britain. And all this at a time when Europe was growing increasingly xenophobic towards refugees from Asia and Africa. Perhaps the difference was that the refugees from Ukraine were white, European and Christian and were being bullied by Russia, still a hate country for many, even after the end of the Cold War. Asian and African students in Ukraine, however, often had a pretty torrid time when they tried to escape via the Polish border; they were not white and probably not middle-class and Christian, 'people like us'.

Many of the Western journalists were also mainly white and often middle class. They appeared genuinely surprised that a major war had again erupted in Europe. The idea that war is 'too civilized for Europe' is of course unhistorical; the continent had long been the most warlike on Earth. Since 1945 NATO countries have *externalized* their warlike instincts to operate in Korea, Vietnam, Iraq and Afghanistan, etc. Even the many Afghans who had bravely fought alongside British and American troops as interpreters often found their welcome in the UK and North America hampered by bureaucracy while anti-immigrant leaders in Poland and Italy, however, welcomed hundreds of thousands of Ukrainians. All this perhaps proved you needed not just the right colour skin and religion but also the right invader or oppressor.

Americans dropped more bombs on Iraq than the Russians did initially on Ukraine. In the war against the Islamic State the US Air Force is alleged to have destroyed or seriously damaged 138,000 houses in 2017. Tens of thousands of Iraqis were killed but NATO propaganda always had their own troops liberating Iraqis not killing them. Most journalists were embedded or corralled in Baghdad's Green Zone; few stories emerged of heroic resistance to the invaders, unlike the daily resistance stories from Ukraine.

Although sometimes critical stories of Israel's occupation and, especially, settlement building in the West Bank emerged, most Western media outlets have not reported Palestinian resistance and Israeli occupation with the same industriousness as Ukrainian women making Molotov cocktails to throw at Russians during the initial envelopment of Kyiv.

Coverage of wars in Vietnam and Iraq led to large scale anti-war protests in Britain and America. But paradoxically the non-stop coverage of the Russo-Ukraine war has led generally to demands for *more* support and *more* weapons to be sent to Kyiv. There was a majority demand in opinion polls at the start of the war for NATO to enforce no-fly zones over Ukraine, as it had in Iraq. But it took a while for the inevitable results of what that policy would create to become obvious – a direct war between NATO and Russia. The mood gradually changed as the war dragged on. Initially, the mood could perhaps be summarized as 'let's see what they can do with all the weapons we have sent and hope the Ukrainians soldiers we have trained actually perform'. The failure of the summer 2023 offensive discouraged more NATO involvement and demands for peace increased at the same time as the cost of living increases, partly caused by the war and energy embargoes, took their toll on Joe Public.

All wars inspire fake news, even the Snake Island heroics at the start of the war. The eighty-two defenders who told the Russian warship to 'fuck off' were killed. And their cheek became a popular meme with T-shirts galore. Moscow, however, insisted they had surrendered and were in custody. Kyiv had posthumously honoured the 'dead' men. A mistake or fake news or a mix of both? In turn the Russians withdrew under military pressure from the island. They called it a 'goodwill gesture' but the Ukrainians claimed it was a victorious battle. And there was the case of the 'Ghost of Kyiv' who was supposed to have been flying a Mig-29 and to have shot down six Russian planes before being brought down himself. One of the various pictures of the pilot was actually alleged to be that of an Argentinian lawyer who could not fly. Yet this story did fly around the world. The Ukrainian Ministry of Defence did admit that it had been propaganda and a useful morale booster at a difficult time. The same had happened in the First World War; various supernatural entities were alleged to have been sighted, from medieval bowmen to the 'angels of Mons'. They were supposed to be protecting British troops.

The Russians no doubt committed many acts of murder, torture and rape around Kyiv especially in Bucha. Both sides have bombed hospitals and schools, a war crime, as are all deliberate attacks on civilians. Many of the crimes will be fully investigated after the war, although the US has been a master of fake news, ever since the deployment of the false story of Iraqi troops tearing babies from incubators in Kuwait. Increasingly, Europe has shut down pro-Russian media such as RT (formerly Russia Today) and Sputnik. The former US Marine and UN weapons inspector, Scott Ritter's views on false-flag operations including some of the rape accusations at Bucha have been censored on some social media. Meta, which owns Facebook and Instagram, and YouTube have blocked pro-Putin material.

Nothing in the West compares with the crackdown on free speech in Russia. The propaganda was that Russian soldiers were fighting fascists just as they did in the Great Patriotic War, and that civilians were not targeted. Within a month of the invasion, criticism – that is, creating 'fake news' about the army or citing Ukrainian sources or even using the word 'war' – could technically land the perpetrator with fifteen years in jail. All independent news sources were shut down or their teams left the country. The remaining bastions of freedom, such as the radio station *Ekho Moscovy* and the TV channel *Dozhd* were closed. 'The Russian media became an echo chamber of lies,' as Philip Short noted in his magisterial biography of Putin. The internet was subjected to draconian controls.

Alexei Navalny, the country's leading jailed dissident, was given even more years in prison on trumped-up charges. Some news got through on the internet, especially from independently minded Russians who had sought exile in the Baltic states. Some Russians did protest in the streets but in relatively small numbers: many held up small sign saying 'No War'; some were arrested even for holding up *blank* signs. Young women as well as the elderly were beaten up by arresting officers. First offenders could be fined, but two arrests in a year could lead to prison time. Then all protesters could go to prison for two years and the banners disappeared, as did the protests. Many chose exile, especially men under 27 who wanted to avoid conscription. Some well-known chess and sports stars and musicians also protested especially when they went into exile.

Many liberals went into exile but others argued that it was better to be a Putin martyr like Navalny. That prevented the Kremlin from saying that all the 'traitors' had been driven into exile. Some opponents in exile say that it was hard to organize any opposition campaigns from a prison, though the film *Navalny* attracted worldwide attention. The main opposition leaders in Belarus, not in jail, created an effective government in opposition in Vilnius. Navalny insisted, bravely and perhaps foolishly, that his place was in Russia even if it had to be a prison cell.

In all wars the bravest are conscientious objectors and special forces. Sometimes they can be the same individuals. Some army soldiers and men in the National Guards either refused to deploy at all or return to Ukraine after one tour. Some of the soldiers were kicked out of the army but a court martial was difficult because, under Russian military law, the country had to be at war for troops to be obliged to fight. Since it was a 'special military operation' soldiers – technically – could not be forced to deploy. But some men were sent to military prison for minor offences such as being absent without leave.

Perhaps up to 80 per cent of Russians supported both Putin and the war effort, especially those who consumed the state-controlled TV; more independently minded Russians tended to use the internet if they could access signals from the Baltic states, for example. Clearly many Russians were rallying around the flag and genuinely believed that Putin was defending the homeland against NATO encroachments. Whether the death toll begins to undermine Putin's ratings partly depends on how the war progresses and for how long. Whether a powerful mothers' lobby will emerge in a replay of the war in Afghanistan is uncertain, even though some mothers whose sons have been killed have publicly asked why.

In the West, the media tended to portray the Russian president as a mad dictator. But you weren't put in a British prison, say, if you described him as a rational nationalist defending his homeland from an over-mighty US-led alliance.

Ukraine has never been free of censorship and the various governments controlled pro- or anti-Russian views according to the political hues of the Kyiv administrations or the location, especially in the Donbas. After the invasion Kyiv cracked down on pro-Moscow websites and broadcasters.

Firehose of Falsehood[1]

Although Russia appears to have abandoned Soviet-era efforts to spread an ideology, it is still interested in popularizing its worldview and raising its esteem in the eyes of international audiences. And the invasion of Ukraine has completely re-focused Moscow's propaganda.

One of Putin's constant themes has been that the war in Ukraine is part of a spiritual battle against the whole of the depraved West. It is no longer the home of ruthless capitalism but of 'sex changes, the rampages of drag queens, barbaric gender debates and an LGBTQ takeover'. Putin argued that there was 'denial of patriotism and the destruction of the traditional family through the promotion of non-traditional sexual relations'.

The Russian government has become far more successful at manipulating social media and search-engine rankings than previously, boosting lies about Ukraine's military with hundreds of thousands of fake online accounts. The Russian operators of those accounts boast that they are detected by social networks only about 1 per cent of the time.

Russia deploys a wide range of tools including the internet, social media, amateur journalists and large trolling farms full of bots and human experts. They shamelessly deploy lies and half-truths on a wide number of channels to overwhelm the audience, both at home and abroad. Media operations in the West try to be truthful, credible and consistent, at least in theory.

Russian propaganda includes text, video, audio and still imagery via the internet, social media, satellite TV as well as traditional broadcast channels. Also, the Russian state uses paid internet trolls who attack or undermine oppositions in online chat rooms, discussion forums and comment sections on websites. Radio Free Europe/Liberty reports that

> there are thousands of fake accounts on Twitter, Facebook, Live Journal and VKontakte maintained by Russian propagandists. According to a former paid Russian internet troll, the trolls are on duty 24 hours a day, in 12-hours shifts, and each has a daily quota of 135 posted comments of at least 200 characters.

RT (formerly Russia Today) has been one of the primary multi-media providers. It broadcasts in English, French, German, Spanish and several Eastern European languages and it is popular online. RT has sometimes provided a useful antidote to pro-NATO propaganda. Russian propaganda, however, has a quantity that has a quality of its own. It is also quick off the mark, not least because it does not verify information in detail as the BBC boasts it does. Stories that Islamic State fighters were joining Ukrainian forces, for example, were put out as disinformation and sometimes many Western media or social media memes pick them up. People tend to accept the first version of a story no matter how many rebuttals are made. Even with impossible stories or urban legends, those who have heard them multiple times are more likely to believe that they are true.

Russian propaganda has the speed and agility to be often first on a story, which affords propagandists the ability to create the first (and often more lasting) impression. The combination of high volume, multiple channels and continuous messaging enabled Russian memes more likely to be familiar to their audiences. This gives them a boost in terms of perceived credibility, expertise and trustworthiness.

The Russians often use credible sources but twist them. For example, RT stated that the famous security expert and blogger Brown Moses (a staunch critic of Assad's regime in Syria whose real name is Eliot Higgins) had provided analysis of footage suggesting chemical weapon attacks on 21 August 2013 had been perpetrated by Syrian rebels. Higgins's analysis, however, concluded that the Syrian government was responsible for the attacks and that the footage was faked to shift the blame.

Why are these fake stories believed? Partly ignorance, especially about technical issues such as chemical warfare, or laziness by journalists let alone couch potatoes at home. Also, most internet users suffer from data overload. And in times of crisis especially, ordinary people in war zones will believe what they want to believe, particularly if the information is coming from their own government. This is called 'information bias'. People tend to view news and accept opinions that confirm existing beliefs as more credible than other news and opinions, regardless of the quality of the arguments. Sometimes it is easy to believe a conspiracy theory because it carries a simple truth – apparently. The perceived presence of evidence can override the effects of source credibility on veracity of statements. For example, in courtroom simulations witnesses who provide more details – even very trivial details – are judged to be more credible.

This is why Russian faux news channel propaganda channels, such as RT and Sputnik, are insidious. Visually they look like news programmes, and persons appearing on them are presented as journalists and experts, making audience members much more likely to ascribe credibility to the information these sources are disseminating.

And yet removing these channels, from British TV access at least, does mean that alternative viewpoints are denied and this implies a censorship that is not, however, in the same league as Moscow's crackdowns.

One important failure of Russian propaganda is the lack of consistency. One well-known example was the constant flip-flops about the downing of the Malaysia Airlines Flight 17. Moscow offered so many explanations, usually inconsistent and always implausible. To cite another infamous example, Putin, insisted that the 'little green men' in Crimea were not soldiers but he later admitted that they were. Another egregious inconsistency is about the funding of the Wagner Group. For years the president denied that the Russian government was funding the mercenaries. Then, when they mutinied, he admitted publicly that the money had come from the state treasury. Telling lies repeatedly, especially on national/international television, can come back and bite politicians in all countries. But, in times of war, information credibility can cost or save lots of lives.

'A lie can travel halfway around the world while the truth is still putting on its boots.' Even that aphorism is not thanks to Churchill or even Mark Twain, but – arguably – Vergil, thousands of years earlier. How many readers will check that out – true or false? This suggests that the idea of countering the firehose of falsehood with 'a squirt gun of truth' is a touch optimistic.

Domestic textbook warfare

Russian schoolchildren have been taught 'fundamentals of life safety classes' for some time. Kids were taught how to deal with terrorist attacks or how to respond to Chernobyl-type poisoning, and more recently online safety. Now pupils over 16 are taught how to assemble and clean an AK-47 as well as combat first aid. In new briefing packs, students are expected to learn the duties of soldiers in combat zones. They will also learn how to operate unmanned drones. A problem may be that many schools will not be able to afford drones to practise with.

The militarized skills will apply not only to sixth-formers but right across the country from primary up a new syllabus will have an emphasis on the defence of the Motherland, patriotism and respect for the Russian language. Revised history courses will enable students to rebut foreign falsifiers of Russian history. The education authorities have been open that the new syllabus is about fighting an information war against the West. The purpose is to instil patriotism in the young.

Discussion of the 'special military operation' is included. Some teachers who have opposed the changes have been sacked and accused of 'discrediting the army'.

It is not hard to understand why Putin wants to persuade students to pass seamlessly from school to the barracks. He has changed at both ends the ages for conscription. From January 2024, students from 18 to 30 will be required to carry out a year of national service. It may be increased to two years if the Ukraine conflict sucks in more cannon fodder.[2]

A British journalist's perspective

The BBC's Steve Rosenberg has covered Russia for decades and has managed, so far, to keep his work visa. Foreign correspondents used to be accredited on one-year visas. That has now been reduced to three months, making it easier for the Kremlin to expel them. He said: 'I've lived here for more than half my life and it's changed. That's hard to deal with - the Russia I thought I knew has gone.' And it has got much tougher since the Ukraine war.

> Russia will always deny it [actions in Ukraine that kill civilians]. Russia will always present itself as the victim and not the aggressor … . Living in this is psychologically draining – a kind of *Alice Through the Looking Glass/Nineteen Eighty Four* Orwellian world.[3]

When asked how much the Russian public absorbed the Kremlin propaganda, Rosenberg said that after the fall of the USSR, people felt they had the power to make changes. Now they believed they could not change their country at all, and this benefits the Kremlin.

> What they think about the war is divided into three parts. You've got maybe 15 per cent who are vehemently pro-war and at the other end of the scale you've got about 15 per cent who are totally against it but don't come on to the streets to protest because it's too dangerous. The vast majority are in the middle.

Interestingly Rosenberg said that the Wagner mutiny has led to a turbocharged Putin. 'He's here, there and everywhere trying to show that he's loved.'

Patriotic branding

How do you brand and market a war that is being so bitterly fought? Books, films and art have celebrated a range of recent events from the defence of Snake Island to the sinking of the *Moskva*. Some of the 'art', such as farmers using their tractors to tow away Russian tanks and APCs, went viral at the start of the war.

But how do you mix profit and patriotism without being tacky? You can buy war memorabilia of everything from vodka to socks and underwear. Ukrainians are understandably keen to buy local goods that announce that a percentage will go to the war effort though, of course, that doesn't always happen. Some soldiers say all the war-junk undermines what they are going through. The government says it will bring in a law to stop racketeering and manipulating patriotism, though many firms are genuinely doing their bit for the war effort. Many military necessities, especially medical aid and drones and ambulances are being funded from private sponsorship. One way of sorting the problem may be to force companies to publish what they voluntarily contribute to the war effort.

It is said that Ukrainian society is divided between those, and their families, who are fighting and those who feel guilty about not doing so. If wearing boxer shorts with a Ukrainian flag satisfies both sides then why not? Whatever the parliament says, Ukrainians will no doubt continue to shop for victory.

Chapter Twelve

Give Peace a Chance?

A forever war in the centre of Europe can benefit no one.

This war seemed senseless to many and yet justifiable to many others, a majority on both sides – perhaps. As Noam Chomsky put it, there was 'criminality and stupidity on the Kremlin side, severe provocation on the US side'.[1] The French especially tried to keep contacts alive with Putin, reminding some American hardliners of their insult during the Iraq wars of the French being 'cheese-eating surrender monkeys'; although longer term perhaps Paris was correct about the fiasco in Iraq. Germany, too, and sometimes Italy tried to keep communications open. But President Biden's comment that 'Putin cannot remain in power' made peace negotiations more complex.

Was Russia's existence really at stake? And was the (unlikely) return of all Ukrainian territories, especially Crimea, worth the Western alliance risking a nuclear war? How long would the voters of Western Europe tolerate the costs to their own pockets, let alone the nuclear risks? Once the decapitation strategy of seizing Kyiv had failed, it appeared that Putin believed that, even short of a convincing military victory, he could wait out the decadent and corrupt West. Time was on the grandmaster's side, he thought.

By August 2023, stalemate seemed built into the conflict. The Ukrainian much-touted summer counter-offensive certainly appeared to have stalled. The losses were almost catastrophic on both sides. And the likelihood of a nuclear accident at a nuclear power station or by a stray missile or, God forbid, a targeted tactical nuclear weapon grew by the day.

But all wars end. Sometimes in negotiation as in 1918 or as a permanent armistice as in Korea. May 1945 was rare – a total unconditional surrender.

Why do combatants seek peace? The most likely reason is when doubts emerge about whether the war is winnable, although many in the German Nazi leadership believed they could win almost until the end. Or something unforeseen could happen – the assassination of a leader or possibly a popular revolt against the slaughter. Or maybe a powerful deus ex machina – Beijing and Washington jointly issuing a démarche.

Peace talks

Numerous talks have been held. The first attempt was in Belarus after a few days of war. Another two rounds followed. The fourth round was held in Turkey. Russia kept blaming the Western powers for stopping Zelensky negotiating, while Kyiv insisted Putin was merely pretending to negotiate. High-powered negotiators were involved, including Roman Abramovich, the former Chelsea FC owner, and Naftali Bennett, the former Israeli prime minister. Some humanitarian issues were resolved such as on-off evacuations of civilians and later PoW exchanges. In a fifth round, on 21 March 2022, Zelensky called for a direct meeting with Putin. Turkish President Erdoğan said that Kyiv was prepared to renounce any plans for NATO membership and make Russian Ukraine's second language.

On 9 April 2023 Boris Johnson, the British premier, visited the Ukrainian capital and was blamed by the Russians for upsetting the peace talks by calling Putin a war criminal. Some of the war crimes committed in places such as Bucha were just being publicized.

The Chancellor of Austria, Karl Nehammer, went to Moscow in mid-April and spoke to Putin. On 26 April the Secretary General of the United Nations, António Guterres, tried to negotiate separately in Moscow with both Putin and Lavrov. Meanwhile, the Russian foreign minister blotted his copybook by suggesting that Hitler was part Jewish. Putin apologized to the Israeli prime minister for Lavrov's statement during peace discussions. In May the US Secretary of Defense, Lloyd Austin, had a long phone conversation with Sergei Shoigu, his opposite number, the first time they had spoken since the war had started.

In mid-May Putin held a summit with his allies in Kazakhstan, Kyrgyzstan, Armenia, Belarus and Tajikistan to talk about conflict. Even the venerable figure of Henry Kissinger, almost 100, entered the fray. He said that Ukraine should swap territory for peace, the formula once endlessly rehearsed in talks about Palestine/Israel by the American sage: specifically, Crimea and the Donbas were to be exchanged. Zelensky told his co-religionist to take a flying leap. He said straightforwardly, 'Ukrainians are not ready to give away their land, to accept that these territories belong to Russia.'

Mexico also tried the intercede in September 2022. In the same month Zelensky addressed the UN General Assembly in a pre-recorded video. Some of the key points were 'just punishment' of Russia for the crimes committed in Ukraine and territorial integrity and the determination of Ukraine to defend itself. After Putin annexed further parts of Ukraine, Zelensky said he would not hold peace talks while Putin was president.

In October China and India, who had so far refrained from any public criticism of Moscow, called for de-escalation and dialogue. China suggested some vague possibilities for peace while quietly warning Putin not to use tactical nuclear weapons. It was made clear that would not be at all good for Chinese state capitalism.

In October Elon Musk deployed his new acquisition, Twitter (later X), to fly a peace flag. The world's on-off richest man, and world-class eccentric, said that Kyiv could permanently cede Crimea to Moscow, while guaranteeing the water supply from Ukraine. The UN could supervise referenda on territories in eastern Ukraine seized by the Russians. Moscow liked the suggestion but Kyiv did not.

In November 2022 the US Chairman of the Joint Chiefs of Staff, Mark Milley, urged Kyiv and Moscow to find a political solution because he believed the war 'was unwinnable by purely military means'. Milley was the highest ranking officer in the American armed forces. He was also a thinker (Princeton University) as well as a very experienced warrior. He had served in South Korea and was very aware of the so-called 'Korean solution' to Ukraine – division after an armistice. The general had also served in Iraq and observed closely the humiliating scuttle from

Afghanistan. Milley was involved with media publicity about his talking to his counterpart in China, especially after bad intelligence that Beijing had gained about a possible first strike by Washington.

Just before Christmas in December 2022 the Ukrainian foreign minister, Dmytro Kuleba, said that the UN Secretary General should hold a peace summit but added that Kyiv could not invite Putin unless he also faced a court for war crimes. The 43-year-old Euro enthusiast had written a well-known book about disinformation so he must have realized that this call would go unheeded. But he was astute on China: Beijing 'will not allow Russia to collapse because they need a weak Russia to make concessions to China, to provide their resources'.

Lavrov returned to the fray by insisting that peace talks with Ukraine would resume only if Kyiv recognized the annexations by Russia.

Both sides seemed to believe that the war could still be won on the battlefield.

As the weaponization of food continued, in April 2023, the Brazilian head of state, Luiz Lula da Silva, expressed his concern about the global consequences of the war, in terms of food and energy security. He emphasized that it was the poorest regions of the world that were suffering most. He warned Zelensky that he 'could not want everything'. Kyiv should give up Crimea in exchange for peace. But the Brazilian president also told Moscow to withdraw from territory it had seized since the 2022 invasion. He advocated a 'peace club' from developing countries, including Brazil and China. The Brazilian president said that Washington should stop encouraging war.

In April 2023 Foreign Minister Lavrov expanded the war aims. He announced that Russia rejected 'the unipolar world order' led by the USA and warned that future peace talks should focus on a 'new world order'.

He could have added that, as a devout Orthodox Christian, all this might happen when Jesus Christ returned. But perhaps a senior religious figure could really create a miracle. On 30 April 2023 the Pope announced that the Vatican had been busy trying to organize a secret 'peace mission'. Sadly, the Orthodox Christians of various competing stripes in Russia and Ukraine had not been in tune with Rome for over a millennium.

In May 2023 the South African president, Cyril Ramaphosa, announced yet another peace plan. Certainly, North African states were suffering acutely from the supplies of food and fertilizer that were being disrupted by the war. And Moscow was more inclined to listen to leaders such as Ramaphosa because generally the black leadership in South Africa shared a sense of gratitude for Soviet support in the armed struggle against apartheid. A practical manifestation of this had been the recent joint South African and Russian naval exercises. South Africa joined a large African delegation, including, *inter alia*, Egypt, Zambia and Senegal, that visited both Kyiv and Moscow in June. A Russian missile strike hit Kyiv while the African diplomats were visiting, a piece of poor PR by the Kremlin which would have known in detail about the visit. In Moscow, Ramaphosa told Putin that the war had to end; the delegation urged Russia to accept a ceasefire but Putin said that the Ukrainian summer counter-offensive was undermining any possibility of a deal. 'We cannot have a ceasefire when we are under attack.'

In July 2023 the Danish foreign minister, Lars Rasmussen, declared his willingness to host a summit, not least by inviting countries such as India, Brazil and China. At the same time his namesake, the former prime minister, Anders Rasmussen, was advocating that NATO countries should send volunteers to Ukraine to help the beleaguered troops there. True, Rasmussen had been an adviser to Zelensky but individual military volunteers from Western countries could be dangerous if they came in large numbers; many had already gone to Ukraine and a few had been killed or captured and used as propaganda by Moscow. If Rasmussen's idea was taken up on a large scale then there could be a replay of Chinese 'volunteers' in the Korean conflict. That was surely the way to full-scale European war.

Indonesia also weighed into the debate suggesting a ceasefire and establishing a demilitarized zone monitored by UN peacekeeping forces. The Ukrainian defence minister, Oleksii Reznikov, intervened. Reznikov, a lawyer from Lvov who had served in the Soviet air force, said that the Indonesian, Brazilian and Chinese plans were 'mediators on Russia's side'. They were not impartial, he said. China could be an effective mediator for peace talks if Beijing could convince Russia to withdraw from all the territories it had occupied.

Saudi Arabia had also been active in peace negotiations. In early August 2023, Zelensky returned to attend a summit in the desert kingdom, as with forty other major players, including the EU and US. Russia was not invited but China was and indeed came. China had previously proposed a twelve-point plan at the UN which included a ceasefire and security guarantees for Moscow while insisting the NATO weapons pouring in were exacerbating the crisis.

In March 2023 China's foreign minister, Qin Gang, said, 'The Ukraine crisis seems to be driven by an invisible hand pushing for protraction and escalation of the conflict.' The minister, who had previously served as Ambassador to Washington, presumably was referring to the USA. Qin Gang, however, suddenly disappeared; he became a non-person in the Orwellian sense. He was in the job for just 207 days, the shortest period for a foreign minister in the history of China. Despite his sound connections with the Americans, and British, there was not a whisper of spying. Apparently he had an affair with a Hong Kong journalist, despite being married with one child. Many in the Chinese hierarchy take mistresses but the affable Qin Gang must have flaunted his affair.[1]

In the West the general consensus in the foreign ministries was that the Chinese were not pressurizing the Russians to make peace. The US believed that the Chinese were trying to freeze the war, to Russia's benefit. Perhaps, like Moscow, Beijing was playing a waiting game. China has benefitted from the cheap energy from Russia and had avoided any sanctions from any overt military backing for Russia. Provided nothing extreme occurred, such as a 'demonstration' of a tactical nuclear weapon, time could indeed be on China's side. Ukraine could become another frozen war, as in Korea, which China has finessed for exactly seventy years.

The French – or at least *a* Frenchman – made a bid for peace in August 2023. Ever since the 1960s and President Charles de Gaulle's well-known suspicion of the 'Anglo-Saxons', especially the Americans, many French voters have shared the notion of a 'special relationship' between

Moscow and Paris. More than a decade after he left the presidential palace, Nicolas Sarkozy gave very pro-Putin interviews to promote his new memoir. He called on Ukraine to accept the Russian occupation of Crimea and other disputed territory; he rubbed salt in the wound by saying Ukraine should not be allowed to join NATO or the EU and should remain neutral to appease Moscow's fears of being encircled by hostile neighbours. The former prime minister of Estonia, Toomas Hendrik Ilves, although a former diplomat, used very undiplomatic language in response by tweeting: 'He's France's most mendacious postwar foreign policy president. On Russia, he's venal as hell. Why should I take this clown seriously?'[2]

Could the French be right again?

Chapter Thirteen

Give War a Chance

While world leaders struggled to find a path to peace, perhaps the majority of the top brass in Moscow and Kyiv believed that the war could still be won. It is a little known part of the Second World War that secret talks were held between Nazi and Soviet negotiators to reach a separate peace late in the conflict, even though Stalin harangued the Western leaders that they should not do the same. And yet the Germans clung to the view that they still had the upper hand even after their Stalingrad disaster. The Nazis simply believed that the master race could never be beaten by Slav *Untermenschen*. In the Russo-Ukrainian war all the leaders were Slavs – often first-language Russian speakers with similar cultural backgrounds; and some had been in the same universities and served together in the Red Army. But Putin did not accept that the Ukrainians had created a separate state; they were 'little Russians'. Putin's war, however, had really forged a fiercely independent state even if there had been some ambiguity before, especially amongst some Russian speakers.

Putin expected a quick victory, but it became a long war of attrition, with some unintended consequences.

One of the war's most acute observers, Professor Lawrence Freedman, summed up how Putin had listened to intelligence he wanted to hear from his cowed advisers in a small cabal: 'This routine manipulation of the truth meant that Putin had become trapped by a false narrative he had helped to form.' Freedman said of the Russian military top brass:

> They would not have been inclined to offer unwelcome advice, even if it had been sought. The incentives to offer only welcome advice permeated the command structure. This meant that few would have

been inclined to point out that the Ukraine operation depended on equipment with parts lost to corrupt practices, or just shoddily maintained, or that the Russian army had not developed tactical concepts to cope with the defensive measures that the enemy was likely to adopt or that insufficient intelligence had been gathered even to work out what these measures might be. If the operation had been the walkover expected, then none of this might have mattered. But it wasn't, and it did.[1]

The Air War

Against nearly all predictions, the mighty Russian Air Force did not secure air supremacy very early on. Nearly all the figures for aircraft shot down are dubious for both sides but, by September 2022, Kyiv claimed that they still had 80 per cent of their air force operational and had shot down fifty-five Russian military aircraft. Right at the start, the significant number of MANPADS – shoulder-launched ground-to-air missiles – had destroyed a large number of Russian helicopters.

Without proper air cover the Ukrainian counter-offensive of June 2023 struggled to be effective – one of the reasons why Zelensky became an, understandably, world-class bore with his demands for F-16 fighters. NATO members did help with pilot training but the American fighters did not appear in the Ukrainians skies in the first year of the war.

What was strikingly new in the war was the very extensive use of aerial drones. Many of them were manufactured in Iran and Russia bought them from Tehran by the hundreds. The initial count was 400 Shaheed and Mohajer drones. They were relatively easy to bring down but not if used in kamikaze swarms; also, they were comparatively inexpensive. Meanwhile, Israel was said to be assisting Kyiv in missile technology to counter Iran's offensive. The Russians also deployed a wide array of their own missiles, both Soviet and more recent weapons including hypersonic versions such as the *Kinzhal*, allegedly capable of flying at Mach 10. They were mostly aimed at infrastructure to knock out water and electricity supplies but they also hit hospitals and railway stations throughout the country, even as far west as Lviv and the Polish border. The Ukrainians also launched drones to hit Russian cities and military bases but never in the quantity to match their enemy. But, especially in hitting Russia, this was a powerful propaganda weapon, not least to display this was a major war, not just the cliched 'special military operation'.

Numerous small tactical drones, often off the commercial shelf, were used by the Ukrainians to drop grenades on the enemy trenches but also to act as recce for the artillery and for bomb damage assessments. The Russians claimed that they knocked out around 100 Turkish Bayraktar TB2s. In the beginning of the war the aircraft could be used for surveillance or were weaponized. The word 'Bayraktar' means 'flag-bearer' in Turkish and the weapons, purchased before the war started, certainly had a major iconic role in the first weeks of the defence of Kyiv.

The Russians have mostly learnt from their initial drone mistakes and have been deploying pairs of drones during the summer Ukrainian counter-offensive: one to spot and one to attack their opponents. The Russians have also got much better at jamming Ukraine's drones. That is why Kyiv is losing perhaps 1,000 drones a month. Replacing them has been way beyond their bureaucratic and corrupt procurement process and so a very versatile private system has been producing some drones for as cheaply as £300 for one-use surveillance versions which can drop grenades. Drone-makers have made, for example, the Sirko and then sold them to better-off compatriots who donate them to the army. Sirko can transmit video for about fifteen miles and can fly overall for forty miles on one battery charge. And it is clever enough to turn off its own GPS when it needs to fly back to its base.

In contrast, Britain had spent many millions on the Thales-supplied Watchkeeper drone. It had just under forty-five of these much troubled machines 'flying' in mid-2023; because of the crashes most were in store. These surveillance aircraft didn't like bad weather at all and have proved to be a white elephant for the army. Army engineers should have made their own small ones themselves or bought them cheaply from a shop and saved a fortune. With their long history of aircraft design, the Ukrainians have been very inventive at this tactical level. The British also operate the far more effective and strategic Reaper MQ-9 drone from RAF Waddington, deploying it in Afghanistan and against the Islamic State. This is perhaps the most lethal drone on earth. America's more advanced types, which can now land on carriers (with the short take-off and landing version) are proving increasingly versatile.

Naval drones

The Ukrainians have also used unmanned naval drones to attack Russian shipping with UK and US assistance. Naval drone technology is evolving fast and may change the future of sea warfare. Sea drones are small and can operate on or below the water's surface. They can be used for clearing mines, surveillance or targeting enemy ships.

Often sea drones feature built-in explosives and cameras that beam images to the controller. Long-range targets are typically pre-programmed into the drone when launched. Costs vary, although the Ukrainian government said that one of its drones had a price tag of just under £200,000; this is cheaper than many long-range missiles.

Using open sources, the BBC estimated that Ukraine has carried out at least eleven attacks with sea drones, including targets in Sevastopol harbour in October 2022; this was the first time in history that both sea and aerial drones were deployed together. CNN also said that sea drones were used to attack the Kerch Bridge in July 2023.

They are inexpensive and are harder to detect on radar because they travel so low in the water and make far less noise. They have disadvantages; for example, communications with the controller sometimes break down or the on-board sensors may have a narrow field of vision that can make tracking moving targets difficult.

This is all still experimental; nevertheless, despite its small navy, Ukraine has managed to stop Russia completely dominating the Black Sea.

So this was the first major drone war of the twenty-first century, in the air and on the sea. Drones plus AI portend a dangerous future.

Conventional War at Sea

Turkey enforced the 1936 Montreux Convention that sealed off Russian warships not registered on their Black Sea home bases. This restricted Moscow replenishing its Black Sea Fleet from outside. The first major naval incident was the scuttling of the *Hetman Sahaidachny*, the Ukraine navy's flagship, in Mykolaiv on 3 March 2022 to prevent it being captured by the Russians. The Russians later captured other Ukrainian ships. The Ukrainians also sank two Russian warships in a missile attack on 24 March.

Many African nations were facing major food shortages and even starvation because of the closure of grain shipments from Ukraine. The International Maritime Organization tried to create a safe sea corridor for commercial vessels to leave Ukrainian ports not controlled by the Russians. Moscow agreed to create a corridor eighty miles long and three miles wide, through its Maritime Exclusion Zone. Ukraine had also laid sea mines in port approaches. Naturally, the Russian foreign minister, Sergey Lavrov, blamed Ukraine's mining for the problem of access for grain ships.

The biggest naval disaster for the Russians was the sinking of a cruiser, its flagship *Moskva*. It was struck by two Ukrainian Neptune anti-ship cruise missiles that set the ship on fire which in turn caused an explosion of its ammunition. Most of the crew were evacuated and the ship was being towed towards Sevastopol for repairs but the Russian ministry of defence said it had sunk under tow in bad weather. The Americans had provided battlefield targeting intelligence, it was later revealed. The destruction of the *Moskva* flagship is one of the largest warships sunk in combat since 1945; the Argentine *General Belgrano*, sunk by the Royal Navy in the Falklands War in 1982, was marginally larger.

Moscow claimed that it had launched retaliatory missiles strikes against the missile factory in Kyiv that had produced the Neptune missiles. The Ukrainian subsonic weapon, the R 360 Neptune, with a range of up to 280 kilometres, was itself based on the original Soviet system, the Kh-36.

Ukrainian naval assets and two low-flying Su-2 aircraft helped to secure the recapture of Snake Island in June 2022. Kyiv also claimed to have destroyed a Russian *Serna*-class landing craft.

Nuclear war?

The threat of nuclear war is now the greatest danger facing the world. It could cause an immediate world catastrophe far far worse than the current 'global boiling'. Russia and the US possess around 13,000 of the world's 14,000 strategic nuclear warheads. All the other nuclear states own just a handful of nukes compared with the old superpower rivals' arsenals. Ukraine is at war with Russia but NATO is also fighting a proxy war with Moscow and its allies, including China and Iran, let alone North Korea. This proxy war could easily lead to direct war, by accident – perhaps a stray missile going into NATO territory or by a big Chernobyl-style incident in a Ukrainian civilian nuclear plant. Or intentionally if Moscow fired a tactical nuclear weapon in Ukraine, as per Russian doctrine. Any use of the most 'tactical' of nukes could very rapidly escalate to a strategic spasm response and a nuclear winter. The balance of terror in the world of mutually assured destruction is different from the 1960s, because most of the leaders then had known war at first hand and had also learned the vocabulary of deterrence. Today's leaders are mostly military virgins and also many systems are becoming dangerously autonomous. They are not run by artificial intelligence yet but they soon could be. Also, some of the Russian strategic nuclear systems are probably dysfunctional because they are old and have not been properly maintained.

Dmitry Muratov, Russia's Nobel-winning journalist said, 'We see how state propaganda is preparing people to think that nuclear war isn't a bad thing. On TV channels here [in Russia] nuclear war and nuclear weapons are promoted as if they're advertising pet food.' The former editor in chief of *Novaya Gazeta* added:

> They announce, 'We got this missile, that missile, another kind of missile'. They talk about targeting Britain and France; about sparking a nuclear tsunami that washes away America.' Why do they say this? So that people here are ready.

So far, the USA is the only country in the world to *use* atomic weapons – twice – as an act of war, in anger. Just as Moscow's military planners fear

NATO expansion, they also do not trust America's no-first use of nukes. US presidents have dismantled many of the nuclear safeguards to stop nuclear war; both Republicans and Democrats have been guilty, from Bill Clinton to Donald Trump. In effect, Washington has removed restrictions on the American right to risk a first strike, not just if continental America is in very great danger but also including a threat to its vital interests or one of its NATO or Pacific allies.

Russia has undoubtedly been sabre rattling in the current war. Putin was quite clear when he said in June 2020:

> The Russian Federation reserves the right to use nuclear weapons in response to the use of nuclear weapons or other weapons of mass destruction against it and/or its allies ... and also in the case of aggression against the Russian Federation with the use of conventional weapons when the very existence of the state is put under threat.

Putin has referred to the use of Russian nukes on a number of occasions since the start of his invasion of Ukraine.

The 12:1 imbalance of military spending between America and Russia has the inadvertent effect of increasing Russia's reliance on its nukes because its conventional forces are much more limited than Washington's. Russia obviously has military superiority in the Ukraine region and technically 'escalation dominance' in the short to medium term, but a long war that could suck in more NATO conventional weapons could mean that Moscow could run out of conventional military options relatively soon compared with the USA. Weapons and manpower shortages are already very apparent in Russia and even in the US ammunition supplies have run very low; hence the reluctant use of cluster munitions.

Both Russia and the USA have had tactical nuclear weapons in their arsenals since the 1950s. Although it was fashionable to talk about waging a tactical nuclear so-called 'limited war' in the 'thinking the unthinkable' days of Herman Kahn and Henry Kissinger, no expert today can predict whether the use of a single tactical nuclear weapon would end there. It is not hard to imagine a desperate Putin resorting to a low-yield tac-nuke if he were in danger of actually losing the Ukraine war. Even the often discussed demonstration effect of a tac-nuke, say in the Atlantic Ocean, could cause massive escalation. Whether Moscow is ever backed into such a corner partly depends on NATO policy.

Both sides must have war-gamed the possible use of tactical nuclear weapons but war is inherently chaotic, especially in this sort of high-stakes scenario. Nobody can say that Russia's use of a low-yield nuclear bomb in Ukraine would not lead to Armageddon. Or, perhaps worse, if a nuclear accident at Zaporizhzhia plant pumps Chernobyl-plus amounts of radiation across all of Europe.

Presidents Clinton, Bush, Obama and Trump walked away from numerous nuclear agreements that emerged from the first Cold War. The single remaining pillar of the decades of nuclear arms controls is the New START Treaty that limits Russia and the USA to an equal number of deployed strategic warheads and weapons carrying them. It came into force in 2011 and was about to expire when Joe Biden became president. The two countries agreed to extend the treaty to 2026. Although Barack Obama came into office promising a 'nuclear-free world', he spent $2 trillion on modernizing American nukes and Russia also was busy upgrading its missiles, submarines and aircraft capable of deploying thermonuclear weapons. Both Moscow and Washington could kill us all.

Joe Biden described Putin's nuclear sabre-rattling as 'overt, reckless and irresponsible'. A nuclear war cannot be won and must never be fought. In March 2023, Putin announced plans to instal Russian tactical nuclear weapons in Belarus, though he added that they would remain under Moscow's control. Comforting? Definitely not.

Call-ups

At the end of July 2023, Moscow raised the maximum conscription age by three years. All healthy men from 18–27 could be conscripted for one year of compulsory military service. Now the age is 30. The army calls up men twice a year and the goal is to reach 300,000 twice a year.

Many left Russia but now it is illegal to emigrate once you have had your call-up papers. Before they had to be hand-delivered or posted, but now an e-mail can suffice. Once summoned, failure to turn up can result in fifteen years in jail.

Some men in the age range are afraid of getting involved with any state bureaucracy, especially if e-mail addresses are required. One young man said, 'I am afraid even if I book to go to the dentist, they can catch me and send me to war.'

At the start of the war, Putin promised that conscripts would not take part in the fighting but that promise has not been kept. Initially, conscripts were used to support the border guards on the Russian-Ukraine border but many have been sucked into combat across the border.

Citizens who have been called up but who do not turn up for duty are banned from travelling abroad, nor can they buy or sell property and even their driving licences can be invalidated. All this compulsion is hardly 'rallying around the Russian flag'. Though social and family pressure also enforce compliance perhaps as the threat of white feathers did in the UK in the Great War.

Many young Ukrainians do not want to fight either, although the sense of national unity appears far stronger than in Russia. In August 2023 Kyiv sacked thirty-three senior conscription officials for taking bribes to not conscript individuals or even in some cases to smuggle them out of the country. In Ukraine all men from 18- 60 are liable for service.

Some young Ukrainians sneak out of the country, mostly via the Carpathian Mountains to Romania. On foot in winter this is a tough journey. Telegram threads give tip-offs on where drafting officers are patrolling. The recruitment officers are dubbed 'Olives' because of the colour of their uniforms. They can hand out notices ordering young men to register at recruitment centres or, sometimes, they are arrested on the spot without a chance to return home. The Defence Ministry claimed it has a proper database where people are given suitable postings, though sometimes recruiters are accused of intimidating tactics and some conscripts complain of being put straight into combat on the front line with just a month's training.

Typically, before this war men who didn't want to do military service would be offered an alternative such as working on a farm or in social services. But that option was removed when martial law was declared. Exemptions do exist – poor health, being a single parent or being a full-time carer. But draft dodgers can face big fines or up to three years in prison. Many do object on genuine pacifist principles. On the other hand, the many military training courses for civil defence do encourage some to join willingly, even if they have not been called up.

As in Russia, the Ukrainians are suffering from high battlefield attrition rates, though the precise figures are kept shrouded in secrecy. Joe Biden once said that corruption was 'kryptonite for a functioning democracy' and Ukraine in particular would have faced massive obstacles to join the EU because of endemic corruption. According to Transparency International's Corruption Perceptions Index, Ukraine ranked 116th out of 180 countries, but its dismal position has improved not least because of NATO concerns that the billions poured in for arms and training is not being misspent. The most corrupt in the world was Somalia, according to Transparency International. In Europe's top ten for corruption, Russia came top, with Ukraine a close second.

Putin's final war?

The Ukraine war was definitely Putin's show. He had been in power for over two decades. He was not a military man, however; he went through minimal reserve training at university then had his national service obligation waived by joining the KGB. But he had done everything to associate himself with a martial image – endless photo-ops sitting in a cockpit as a top gun, waving new guns or driving the latest Russian tank. He was often photographed bare-chested in the wilderness or throwing an opponent in judo or triumphing on the ice-rink. Putin has showcased shamelessly to the image of hard-man Spetsnaz Rambo – though he may never have been under fire in his life.

Putin encouraged the establishment of a military theme park on the outskirts of Moscow. It is a vast temple painted in khaki green on the outside. The entrance steps are made from melted-down German tanks and guns and so visitors are told they are striking a blow against the enemy with every step. One of the president's major themes has been to remind the population that fighting in Ukraine is the same as fighting in the Great Patriotic War.

The wartime German High Command often commented *sotto voce* about the 'Corporal' in charge. But the Führer had earned the Iron Cross and had seen war firsthand at the front for four years albeit at a very low level. Like Hitler in the last years in his bunker, Putin had surrounded himself with a small group of cronies and yes men. Some were competent soldiers such as the Chief of the General Staff, Valery Gerasimov, who was appointed in January 2023 to get a grip on the faltering war. Part of the problem had been Putin's micro-managing. But even a close friend such as Defence Minister Shoigu, who used to holiday with the Boss, was apparently reluctant to nay-say Putin. Shoigu, a popular national figure, had very little actual military experience, despite his uniform with lots of braid and decorations. Putin did listen to his intelligence chiefs especially the Security Council secretary, Nikolai Patrushev; he was a year older than Putin and had previously served as the director of the Federal Security Service from 1999 to 2008. As in the West, especially regarding the invasion of Iraq, intelligence was often bent to fit political demands. At least in London and Washington intelligence chieftains did not run the whole game. They did in Moscow. Like all acolytes in a dictator's inner circle, they tended to tell the president what he wanted to hear, not what he needed to hear.

Putin had isolated himself at an absurd level during the Covid pandemic. It was not only the supersized table so satirized in the Western media. Visitors had to endure two weeks of strict and heavily sanitized isolation before even getting to the big table. Whether Putin was as ill as some suggested (though not the CIA) or whether it was the hyper-health vigilance of a hypochondriac, Putin became even more isolated from normal advisers or even normal life, as he brooded on the possibilities of war with Ukraine. Perhaps in his long isolation he may have thought that illness or mortality would overcome him sooner rather than later. So, it was now or never to be the great hero who rebuilt the greatness of the old empire.

When the war started, Putin had poor central military command. It was very unlike the all-arms centralization of NATO forces. The Russian army seemed riven by rival commanders as well as the idiosyncrasies of militias such as the Wagner Group and Ramzan Kadyrov's Chechens. And the army seemed not to be talking much to the navy and air force, let alone to each other.

As the heavy metal posturing of 140,000 troops turned into an invasion, suddenly the question was asked 'Why' – not just in NATO capitals but in Moscow too. Putin seems to have consulted with his generals at the last minute. His posturing before the war had helped to wreck confidence in the Ukrainian economy. And many of the world leaders had been queueing up to speak to Putin, who loved being in the spotlight. And NATO leaders were mostly putting pressure on Zelensky to do a deal. But what looked like a winning position and common sense to outsiders was viewed differently in the tiny Putin command bubble.

Many Western intelligence experts expected a fairly quick win despite the NATO training from 2014. After all, Ukraine was riddled with corruption as well as fellow travellers with Moscow. The Ukrainian army had performed poorly in 2014. True, a history of previous wars had shown a spirit of resistance, especially as guerrillas. Some of the terrain would suit a replay of, say Afghanistan. So Westen experts looked more at a long insurgency, perhaps aided by the West as in the case of Western support for the Mujahedeen.

Instead, the small regular army fought well and intelligently, as did highly motivated Territorial Defence troops. And the popular support of ordinary citizens – deploying Molotov cocktails and old hunting rifles – right from the start of the defence of Kyiv displayed a skilled and determined resistance. This was really a 'people's war' of revolutionary literature.

Because most Russians, especially the top brass, believed what their boss said, they did not expect much resistance. The Russians changed commanders – a large number were killed by the Ukrainians – and seemed to have up to five separate operational command centres. There were not enough men, ammunition, fuel or food. The general staff had planned a limited police action, not a big war. The Ukraine would not fight to defend their neo-Nazi government, led by a clown (albeit a Jewish clown).

As the short police action turned into the biggest European war since 1945, all the intrinsic flaws in the Russian military machine became obvious: from the basic indiscipline, bullying and neglect by officers to corruption and problems of basic maintenance of vehicles. The army, either to save money or to rake off commission, had bought Chinese tyres instead of heavy-duty military ones. They just fell apart. Out-of-date rations and a lack even of those had been a cause of Russian looting in the beginning of the war. The new military police units recently set up were little in evidence to stop the raping, murder and torture in areas such as Bucha. As an expert on Russian forces put it, Putin had ensured failure,

> by forcing the generals to fight a powerful enemy without proper preparation, without adequate logistics, and to a strategy based on political prejudice rather than facts on the ground ... and the General Staff had presumed that a major land war such as this would be fought with forces bulked out with at least a partial mobilization not, as here, at peacetime strength.[2]

The Soviet war in Afghanistan, and the mothers' movement that helped to bring it to a close, demoralized the Russians forces. And yet, in the first few months of the Ukraine war, Moscow had lost more troops than in ten year years of fighting the Afghans. And many of the best regulars (*Contractniki*) had been killed. Tons and tons of modern equipment, especially tanks, had been destroyed. Moscow did not deploy the much heralded Armata tank, partly because it had so few and the protypes were unreliable and partly because they didn't want one captured, perhaps. Half of the equipment in the beginning was captured or abandoned – having the T-14 Armata paraded through Kyiv would have been very embarrassing. The meme of Ukrainian farmers using their tractors to tow away Russian military vehicles had already gone viral on the internet.

Putin had fostered his revamped military as part of a modern Sparta. But demographic problems, a shortage of young men, as well as the fact that few Russian youngsters wanted to join the army as a career, despite all the media hype about the heroics of Spetsnaz, meant a reliance still on conscription; the plans for a regular all-professional army, as in many Western countries, had not been achieved, partly because the salaries were not good enough. National service could be extended to two years but that would not be popular. And the increase in females (around 39,000) had not filled the gap; though prison reformers say that a Wagner type of recruitments had encouraged some female inmates to join up for battlefield deployment.

Moscow had restored military chaplains in 2009 as part of the movement to merge the ethos of church, state and military. Mainly Orthodox chaplains were recruited though Patriarch Kirill apparently vetoed camouflage cassocks but did allow rabbis and imams to join up.

So far a major popular reaction or formal mothers' movement has not emerged. Crackdowns on anti-war protesters were severe. Whether more and more 'Cargo 200' – military body bags or zinc-lined coffins – inspire more Russian domestic anger, despite all the propaganda, is unknown but the 'Afghan Syndrome' and 'Chechen Syndrome' (PTSD among returnees) may become the 'Ukraine Syndrome'. And this is hard to hide or suppress.

The 16 April 2023 edition of *The New York Times* quoted a Pentagon report which said that Russia had suffered between 189,500 and 223,000 casualties. Those numbers included 35,000 to 45,000 men killed in action and another 154,000–180,000 wounded. Ukraine had suffered between 124,500 and 131, 000 casualties. The Peace Research Institute in Oslo put total Russo-Ukraine war fatalities as 81,000 on both sides in 2022.

Families of dead Russian soldiers can claim up to seven million roubles in compensation – around £70,000 which is a fortune in rural Russia. Technically, if no corpse is returned no money is paid. There have been reports, probably disinformation, of incinerators behind the front line cremating piles of bodies. What is more accurate is the bureaucracy of the bereavement; often coffins are sent months after the death of a soldier. This is very distressing for Orthodox and Muslim families for whom a prompt burial is customary.

Medical evacuations

In modern wars, such as in Afghanistan, British and American combat troops often survive horrific injuries that in earlier conflicts would have killed them. Today rapid 'medevacs' and prompt front-line hospital treatment save many lives. This is not always the case in Ukraine. Putin may have used the war to empty his jails but Kyiv believes it is often losing its brightest and best who volunteer to fight. Ukrainian troops have been dying in their hundreds, if not thousands, because of poor or slow medical provision, especially during the summer offensive. Ukrainians know that the attrition is high and many are volunteering for independent front-line medical units. Because Ukraine does not have air supremacy, the military can rarely deploy helicopters as is common in NATO operations. Combat medics can take up to four to five hours to rescue a wounded man from the front line and it can then take up to five hours to go from battlefield first aid stations to more advanced medical assistance in urban hospitals. That's too long for severe wounds. Understandably, the West has contributed the weapons Kyiv has been crying out for, but not enough medical aid, especially all-terrain ambulances.

And the medical kits are sometimes low-grade. The Ukraine Medical Forces Command has been involved in corrupt procurement to provide low-grade Chinese medical kits, especially with almost useless tourniquets, a key part of initial medical responses; a large number of American medical kits have also gone AWOL. Disturbingly, some of the medical aid donated by the West is almost or actually out of date. Ineffective Chinese tourniquets cost perhaps around £2 while a first-class American version costs £35. Numerous injured troops die from blood loss in the time it takes to get to hospital. Hence the vital need for reliable tourniquets. (For more details on this story, see Svitlana Morenets, 'Ukraine's Killing Fields', the *Spectator*, 26 August 2023.)

The West often forgets how sovietized Ukraine still is. The bureaucracy, for example, of getting a replacement for an ambulance destroyed by Russian shelling or mines is hard to fathom for modern NATO planners. Technically an ambulance is not registered as being destroyed until an official investigation has taken place and this can take months. Until the paperwork is done the destroyed ambulance stays on the books and no replacement comes. Despite state red tape and corruption, many Ukrainians are can-do people, so they have raised money for private ambulances and small mobile hospitals in buses. In some hospitals nearer the fighting doctors and nurses dig into their small salaries to buy basics such as antibiotics, and even gloves. Many of the combat medics lack training though the UK has trained about 17,000 Ukrainians, of whom some were medics. Though grateful, some of those who returned to Ukraine explained that the British training focused on gunshot trauma when many of the wounds in Ukraine result from artillery shells – being blown apart.

Ukraine's medics have to be able to use weapons as they are expected to fight if necessary, especially as Russians tend to target medics and ambulances. Russian drones target the red crosses for their artillery.

'Hedgehogs'

Because of the current stalemate and trench warfare of August 2023, many Ukrainian casualties are being caused by landmines along the 600-mile active front. The Russians have placed up to four mines per square metre, making it the largest minefield in the world. Ukrainian sappers work at night with little more than a knife and shovel. The army calls them 'hedgehogs'. In addition, the defence lines contain dragons' teeth anti-tanks obstacles, razor wire, ditches and interlocking manned trenches. Many of the new Western-donated tanks and APCs were torn apart by the minefields. It is now easier to send two to three people at night to quietly clear the mines. It is a lot slower of course; one of the reasons Kyiv gives for the very slow movement of their 2023 summer offensive. These sappers are very brave men. They have to avoid numerous booby traps, some on dead bodies, and some designed to be detonated by the lead sapper with a metal detector. They then have to unthread the mine's fuse using a Ukrainian device called a DZM-1. Besides removing mines, the sappers also lay them. They use some of the explosives recovered to drop them from drones on the trenches in front of them.[3]

Cyber warfare

Before the invasion, Moscow had deployed extensive HUMINT (human spies) as well as cyber resources. Washington expected a massive cyber onslaught if the Russians actually invaded. After 2014 Ukraine had experienced cyber-attacks, including the first in which a power station had been switched off, remotely, in the dead of winter.

The US Cyber Command had assumed Russia would launch a blizzard of cyber-attacks to accompany a physical onslaught, crippling commutations, power, banking and government services. So, in December 2021, a small American cyber team, of about forty led by a major, moved into Kyiv. They initially wanted to check just how much Moscow had already penetrated Ukrainian networks. The Americans call these 'Hunt Forward' missions to help allies. They are 'hunters' who know the behaviour of their Russian prey.

Since 2018, US cyber teams have deployed in twenty countries to help allies in Europe, the Middle East and in the Indo-Pacific region. Exceptions were Britain, Germany and France who had their own extensive expertise.

Some of the operations are aggressive. The most famous example was the co-operation with Israel in Operation OLYMPIC GAMES, to destroy elements of the Iranian centrifuge programme. The cyber offensive against Iran's nuclear plans, especially at Natanz, was ordered by President George W. Bush in 2006 and was accelerated under President Obama. One of the reasons was that the Israelis may well have bombed the nuclear plants if the Americans had not worked closely with them to knock the Iranian plants out by other means. The cyber team in the US called it 'bug'; it later became known in the IT community as Stuxnet. Apparently it worked because it stopped about a thousand centrifuges from functioning. But then an Iranian technician at the Natanz plant plugged in his computer and the virus escaped to contaminate the world.

Other opponents have been state hackers in China and North Korea but Russia has been the most persistent cyber adversary. Ukraine was the first time extensive cyber-attacks had been combined with full-scale war.

Before the invasion, the American cyber teams worked closely with the Baltic states, especially Lithuania. Croatia had also been helped. Even countries close to the US could be nervous, however, about allowing foreign experts to root around in their networks. A decade ago, the revelations of Edward Snowden, a former US intelligence contractor, made it clear that the US spied on friends as well as enemies. So American cyber teams have to be diplomats as well; they have to persuade their hosts that they are there to help them, to scan for threats, not to spy on them. Though suspicions can never be totally dispelled, the great concern about Russian infiltration binds the cyber teams.

The US Cyber Command works closely with the National Security Agency, America's largest intelligence agency that monitors communications and cyberspace. The US teams usually share what they find and then get the partners, in this case Ukraine, to eject the Russian infiltration. The Americans also use commercial tools so that their local partners can continue once the joint mission is over.

A cat-and-mouse game often develops with Russian hackers who are very good at changing tactics. In 2021 the Americans worked out that Russian intelligence was using software from a company called SolarWinds to infiltrate companies and governments who had bought it. The US experts, nearly all in their early to mid-twenties, found where the Russians were hiding malware in the network. They discovered eight examples of malicious software, planted by Russian intelligence. This kind of hunting is not just altruistic. Sometimes a cyber operator can find that malware discovered in an allied network was also present in US government systems.

Once the invasion had happened, the US cyber operators watched in real time as a 'wiper' software hit multiple Ukrainian government websites. Wiper attacks can make computers inoperable. The US operators helped Ukrainian intelligence to counter the threat.

Starlink

The second richest man in the world is also the biggest showman in the world. And yet perhaps he is also the second man, after Zelensky, to have saved Ukraine from defeat. Elon Musk did challenge Putin to single combat, as he later did with Mark Zuckerberg – but in a cage. The South African-born multi-billionaire also challenged the head of the Russian space programme to a fight. In a tweet before he bought Twitter, now X, he posted a picture of himself wielding a flame-thrower and a mocked-up image of bare-chested Putin riding a bear through a river. Despite being the 'saviour' of Ukraine, he also angered their top leadership by saying that peace could be achieved if Putin was allowed to keep Crimea. Famously, the Ukrainian ambassador to Berlin responded: 'Fuck off is my very diplomatic reply to you.'

Musk's game-changing contribution to Ukraine has been a constellation of satellites called Starlink that redefined combat on the ground. Musk's SpaceX company launched these low-orbiting devices in 2019. Musk's wizardry has set up unlimited connectivity on the battlefield. Starlink has been used by Ukraine for communication, such as keeping in touch with the outside world and keeping the energy infrastructure working. The service is also notably used for warfare: communicating with combat aerial drones and naval drones, artillery fire co-ordination systems and attacks on Russian positions. SpaceX has expressed reservations about the offensive use of Starlink by Ukraine beyond military communications and so restricted Starlink communication technology for military use on weapon systems. SpaceX, however, kept most of the service online. Its use in attacking Russian targets has been heavily criticized by the Kremlin, of course.

Musk had warned that the service was costing $20 million per month, though a Ukrainian official (under)estimated SpaceX's total contributions as over $100 million. In June 2023, the US Department of Defense signed a contract with SpaceX to finance Starlink use in Ukraine.

An hour before the Russian invasion, Moscow launched a cyber-attack on Viasat, the US system provider. Ukraine's front-line communications were crippled. So Ukraine's minister of digital information, Mikhailo Fedorov, begged for help from Musk in a tweet: 'While you try to colonize Mars, Russia is trying to occupy Ukraine.' He then asked Musk to provide Ukraine with Starlink stations. Musk replied within hours and provided the links. Within days the dishes (about the size of a pizza box) used to access the satellites began to arrive in Ukraine. The dish could be powered by a cigarette lighter in a car. (Luckily Ukrainians are heavy smokers.) Within a few weeks, tens of thousands of dishes had arrived. Zelensky relied on them for transmitting his nightly message to the nation. Initially, Musk took the hit on all the costs, including the dishes that cost over £400.

The dishes, which Musk or his PR people had dubbed 'Dishy McFlatface', have popped up all over the battlefield. And in the sea. A Ukrainian naval drone was found in the Russian naval base at Sevastopol with a Starlink dish lashed to its stern. Because of the low orbit it does mean fewer software glitches. The 5,000 satellites have in-built systems which gives them evasive capabilities that makes it almost impossible to bring them down. Having failed to jam them, the Russians have been working on a missile that might be able to find and hit them. Normal military satellites can be shot down but the Musk swarms make this more difficult as the ensuing debris field could damage other satellites, including Russians ones.

So Kyiv stopped telling Musk to fuck off; the Ukrainians were too much in hock to the mad genius even if the American tax-payers were afterwards picking up the tab.

Mosaic war

It is Putin's karma that he helped to pioneer asymmetric warfare and what has also been called mosaic war: different weapons systems, both kinetic and using soft power and information warfare as well as cyber power, had ended up as almost a First World War struggle of trenches and artillery and attrition. This means more casualties and could boost more popular discontent about the inevitable economic costs of the war and sanctions.

Russia's future and the outcome of the war may well depend on who is Putin's successor and how he takes over.

Chapter Fourteen

A New Era?

Instead of a more independent Europe with the EU at the helm, the NATO alliance led by Washington had come again to dominate Europe. President Macron had called NATO 'brain dead'; now it was a very active and more powerful alliance, strengthened immensely by the new members with powerful armed forces: Finland and Sweden. Once Ukraine could perhaps have been a bridge between Western Europe and the East. Now the war had left a savage divisive bitterness.

This is precisely what Sergei Lavrov had warned about. The US idea of its hegemony in a unipolar world and 'rule-based' system – *their* rules – had to end. China and Russia would co-operate with the global south and create a much fairer world. They would recruit other members to join their BRICS coalition to lead the global south. When their big summit met in Johannesburg in late August 2023, however, Putin was not there. South Africa had signed up to the International Criminal Court and would have had to arrest him if he had attended the BRICS summit.

'We need to steel ourselves for the long fight ahead.' Joe Biden was talking in terms of a new cold war. The US administration was determined not only to stop the aggression against Ukraine but to deter the Russian threat worldwide.

According to Serhii Plokhy, the doyen of Western experts on Ukraine, the current struggle

> has become the latest military conflict in the long history of wars of national liberation which can be traced back to the American Revolution ... and accompanies the decline and disintegration of world empires ... the first 'good war' since the global conflict of 1939–45.[1]

Professor Plokhy argued that Russia had isolated itself and the Kremlin's attempt to rebuild the glory days of the Soviet Union would collapse along with Putin himself. A coup against Putin may happen – a bigger Wagner mutiny perhaps – but the new strongman in Moscow will probably be far more nationalistic than Putin. More a rabid strongman and certainly no Navalny. Because much of the world supports Russia or is neutral, many in the global south regard NATO as an aggressive alliance. Iraq's tragedies cannot be forgiven, they say.

Plokhy is on more solid ground when he argued that if Ukraine survives 'it will emerge from this war more united and certain of its identity than at any other point in its modern history'. He was also probably correct in suggesting that Russian dominance will fade in the rest of the 'post-Soviet space'.

Despite the easy habit of using Cold War rhetoric this is a new era with many as yet unknown techniques to manage the coming conflict, especially if a direct war between China and America erupts. Instead of a rules-based system, anarchy could emerge even if many in the global south will judge it to be an improvement.

The West is back in action, as many Westerners would argue. The South China Sea is not a Chinese sea and Washington refused to accept Ukraine as part of the Kremlin's near abroad. Washington has extricated itself from Afghanistan – albeit very clumsily. Russia is now sunk in the imbroglio it once wished on America in Vietnam. Washington has formed a very powerful coalition against the Russian war. Not only did Finland and Sweden add powerful armed forces to NATO but it was clear that Moscow could do very little to stop the process.

NATO should not revel too much in *schadenfreude* at Russian military cock-ups. The Alliance made a mess of Iraq and Afghanistan. The British Army lost its two wars in both countries because of poor generals and massive under-resourcing by the government. The intervention in Kosovo did not cost any NATO lives but locals died in large numbers and much of ex-Yugoslavia still is a tinderbox. Libya turned out to be a disaster for most Libyans as well. Usually, Western intervention tends to backfire, despite often good intentions. NATO planners should prepare for the worst but also under their breath say thank God they do not have to be in the front line against the damn Russians. Tough bastards, when cornered, many British military experts may exclaim.

On the other side, Russia might have secured verbal support from the south but its allies in the Collective Security Treaty Organization (CSTO) did not join in. Even Belarus did not join the fight though President Lukashenko had been saved from his own people by Moscow because of a rigged election just a few years before. Moscow did do a deal with isolated Iran, not least to secure drones in exchange for help with Tehran's space programme.

What China does will be key in the new era. It has lost what it thought was a major military ally, but it will also gain from the cheap energy. Plokhy said a 'Great Wall' has gone up between Russia and the West. And that the two rivals to America – China and Russia – have had a role reversal. In the 1950s China was the junior partner, however.

Much of the trajectory of the new era will depend on whether this new dangerous world will generate a China-America war. It matters what China has learnt from the Ukrainian resistance. Could the USA back the Taiwanese in the same way as it did the Ukrainians? Beijing is likely to besiege Taiwan, not invade it. And that is harder to counteract.

China and Russia went into a limited-war posture in the 1960s and this later allowed the Kissinger-Nixon diplomacy to forge a separate deal with Beijing. It became a tripolar world. China has never forgotten that parts of Siberia and the Russian far east were once claimed by China; and more and more Chinese are operating in the sparse Russian eastern territories.

Foreign Minister Lavrov wanted to end the concept of a US-dominated unipolar world but now he has helped to augment a far more dangerous bipolar world of China versus America. Putin wanted to restore Russian greatness but he has merely turned his great country into a lapdog of Beijing.

The new autocrats, especially the Chinese, Russians and North Koreans, all rely more or less on getting popular support from constantly replaying the glories of the past: the great victories against the Germans in Moscow's case, against the defeated Nationalists in Beijing's case and the South Koreans and their imperialist American allies in the case of Pyongyang. Putin, Xi and Kim all manipulate history as 'pom-pom waving' as historian Simon Schama expressed it so colourfully.

Chapter Fifteen

Conclusion

The big hurt is still there

Perhaps the West should have been nicer to the bankrupt forlorn country when the USSR disintegrated under the hapless and drunken leadership of Boris Yeltsin. Although Russian membership of NATO was discussed, no strategic plan crystallized to bring Moscow in from the cold. Whether Russia, especially under an early Putin, could ever have joined is a moot point. Scholars often point out that Putin had written about restoring Russian greatness in a number of essays during his career. Washington, however, did not offer any Marshall Plan Mark 2 or praise the country for its bloodless revolution. Instead, Moscow was smothered in a blanket of American hubristic triumphalism. Just a tiny dose or two of Yankee imperialism could easily irritate European sensitivities, especially of course the ever-touchy French. The USA sent earnest if naïve young graduates from the Harvard Business School and the like to teach poor ignorant Russians how to privatize their industries and how to embrace the glories of Western capitalism. According to Paddy Ashdown, a former Royal Marine, ex-spook and thoughtful former leader of the British Liberal Democrats,

> The result was a bonanza of corruption, the humiliation of the Yeltsin years and a clumsy attempt to expand NATO and the European Union right up to the Russian border. There was always going to be a consequence of this folly and its name is Vladimir Putin.

Effects of the war

Yet the war has also weakened Putin and perhaps made him, and Russia, more dangerous. And the Russian economy has shrunk. Now the Kremlin has to rely more on repression and propaganda rather than better living standards to keep the people content. It's said that Putin's power is vertical but the popular resistance in Ukraine suggests that people power is horizontal there.

And all the sabre-rattling by Moscow has renewed long-forgotten fears of a nuclear war, not just over Ukraine but, *inter alia*, over competition in the Arctic.

The war has been about Ukraine's sovereignty and now its sense of nationhood has been dramatically augmented.

The war has encouraged anxieties about China using the military distraction of NATO versus Russia to seize Taiwan. Does Washington have the stamina for a two-front war? Certainly, the Ukraine war has revived the NATO that President Macron called 'brain-dead' in late 2019. The addition of Finland and Sweden, the polar opposite of what Putin wanted, has forged NATO into an overwhelmingly powerful alliance. It is much more technically capable of fighting a twenty-first-century war, unlike the old god of war, artillery, and cannon fodder style of the old-fashioned Russian strategy.

Germany has buried many shibboleths from the Second World War and has re-armed. The arms dealers are in clover. Japan and South Korea are re-arming big time, too. If a conventional Third World War ever descends, then this time Britain, France and America will be fighting alongside Italy, Germany and Japan.

The energy crisis has fuelled inflation in Europe and also industrial action in the UK. In North Africa the grain embargoes have led to famines.

Migration has become a dominant political imbroglio in Europe, not least because more than 14 million Ukrainians have fled from their homes, though some have returned in the West of the country. Many of the young and some of the best and brightest have left Russia and swollen the diaspora in Europe and America.

And the costs of fossil fuel and dramatic weather conditions have rebooted the green agenda. People are perhaps flying less, partly because the journey can be much longer and more expensive with the closure of Russian and Ukrainian airspace.

And, finally, the trivia: Chelsea football club has got a new owner, after the long reign of Roman Abramovich.

That is a summary of the past. What does the future look like?

The war between Russia and Ukraine will end. And the US-Russian rivalry may wind down, though they may never become good friends. As the dominant global power, Washington has wanted to lead. In short, however, Russia has refused to be led. This would have been true of probably any Russian leader. Waiting for Putin to go is not any kind of long-term panacea because Putin is a symptom, not the cause, of what is wrong in Russia.

Prigozhin said that to win the war against Ukraine Russian would have to be far more like North Korea. The arch *condottiero* was completely wrong. If, finally, Moscow wants to be a real European city it needs to be less rather than more authoritarian. Paris should again be its model, never Pyongyang.

The main problem is that Russia never decolonized but, more to the point, did not de-Stalinize. The once-ruling Communist Party never faced Nuremberg trials as the surviving Nazi leadership did.

Assuming no black swan events intrude such as nuclear mushroom clouds on the horizon, the war in Ukraine may become a frozen war as in Korea. An outright victory is unlikely but not impossible. It may be a negotiated peace. The previous chapter on peace deals makes it pretty clear where a compromise could be reached. Assuming the stalemate drags on for another year or so, exhaustion may set in. Washington and Beijing, if they are not at war themselves, may agree to nudge their sides to compromise.

Peace deal?

To play fantasy peace-making, some variation and combination of the following could work.

1. Despite its aggression, Moscow will get back what it has been Russian territory for hundreds of years: Crimea. The ports could be leased to Kyiv for a big sum in exchange for the canal being open to Crimea to supply water.
2. A large UN-led peacekeeping force will monitor a ceasefire zone as well as supervising a free and fair referendum in the two republics in the Donbas. The UN force will consist of an equal number of troops from NATO and pro-Russian states. BRICS and its new members could be involved.
3. Russia will gradually wind down its forces in the rest of the occupied territories on a five-year timescale that will be matched by a gradual reduction of Western sanctions.
4. The UN will organize the return of PoWs as well as the estimated 1.3 million abducted Ukrainian children.
5. Despite its many faults, the International Criminal Court and/or other new or existing organs will organize an international commission to investigate war crimes on both sides.
6. An EU commission will assist in a reconstruction programme for rebuilding Ukraine, assisted by traditional organizations such as the IMF.
7. NATO will consider a twenty-year period before Ukrainian membership.

This proposal has many loopholes but it is better than continuing the war. It is, like most peace deals, somewhat idealistic and inevitably a compromise. It assumes goodwill and common sense on both sides. If they had been there all along then war would not have broken out, would it?

And hundreds of thousands on both sides have been killed or seriously wounded. Probably it will take generations for the bitterness and anger to subside. Like the Irish, Slavs have long memories – it goes with their long troubled past. And it will depend on the quality of the peacemakers.

Most of all, a real peace as opposed to a ceasefire or armistice, will depend on what happens mainly in Moscow but also in Kyiv. Hard-line ultra-nationalists are prowling in the wings in both capitals. Zelensky may have morphed from a second-rate comic to hemispheric hero but the likelihood of his assassination is as high as his rival's. If there were a hint of concession such as giving up the Crimea, he could be ousted or even 'accidentalized' by right-wing opponents. It is not only Russian private jets that can be brought down.

Washington does not have a good track record with regime change. Iraq is the most egregious example but many other comparisons could apply to Russia. Wagner no doubt weakened Putin's position in the ruling gerontocracy but no one can know if the successor regime will be better or worse, especially regarding the termination of the ghastly war in Ukraine.

The fate of Putin is much more pressing than Zelensky's because he initiated the invasion, no matter what the provocation. Putin liked to compare himself with great Russian historical figures such as Peter the Great. But he could end up as another Tsar Nicholas II who also found himself leading a war he could not win. Putin is now 71 and constitutionally can go on until 2036 when he will be 83. Maybe he may want to retire with some security – he gave Boris Yeltsin and his family a special farewell deal that they would not be prosecuted. Putin will want to protect his second family especially and keep some of his billions. He probably cannot go into exile because many countries will not be able to, or want to, protect him from the ICC or Ukrainian hit squads.

Many members of Putin's coterie are also old. So far Putin has avoided creating an heir, as did Stalin. A possible successor, Nikolai Patrushev, is a year older than Putin. Unless there is a Wagner Mutiny Mark 2, then a slightly younger successor is likely to emerge from the existing ageing security and intelligence elite. A new younger generation could, however, be less sentimental about the old Soviet Union and more concerned with rebuilding Russia after a costly war. They might even be more wary of hanging on to the coat-tails of Beijing. They are not likely to reach out too far to the Kyiv government or the West, but they will be more pragmatic in considering the needs of Russian citizens. They cannot be ignored for ever.

Putin, an avid if sometimes faltering student of history, knows that Russian leaders are rarely deposed by popular protest. Nemesis usually came from their own courtiers. Like Stalin, Putin ruled by balancing rivals off against each other, like a mafia boss – Sopranos on speed. He played them off against each other, paying special attention to rival security organizations making them watch each other and promoting and demoting any heroic general from rising to threaten the autocrat. When the time comes, Putin will be removed by those closest to him. As Tsar Nichol II and Khrushchev found out, military folly can cost the crown. The trigger will come from within the Kremlin bunker.

If the 'men of power' (the *Siloviki*) do decide to act they will face a hydra-headed security apparatus that not even insiders fully comprehend, as the Wagner mutiny displayed.

So what should the West do? It should be careful in what it wishes for. If a Brutus finds Putin off-guard it could be worse for Europe. The Russian president appears sane and has control of the nukes. His fall could break up the federation and his gangster capitalism could lead to gang warfare on a big scale. The Islamic State and its franchises are already busy telling Muslims in Russia's peripheral republics that they should take advantage of the Kremlin's stumbles. The Adolf Hitler argument may apply. It was allegedly an Allied reason for not assassinating him – the Nazi leader was making so many critical strategic errors that getting rid of the Führer might inadvertently create a more successful strategic leadership of the war.

Putin did a good job of rebuilding Russia in his first two terms, but he has destroyed his legacy in the last period of his rule. Maybe his successor will stick to two terms. No castling – no election rigging. Maybe even some of the imprisoned leaders such as Navalny could be freed. Or sent into exile, just like Alexander Solzhenitsyn. And, ironically, he held many of the same nationalist views as Puttin, especially about Ukraine.

The Tsarist empire dissolved within months. The USSR broke up in three days. The Putin 'vertical tower' may crumble in hours.

It is often said that the war in Ukraine was morally a 'good war' for the West, especially after Vietnam and Iraq. No war is good. It is a failure of diplomacy and of the human spirit. All wars are pointless, particularly in this era of plentiful nukes and a 'boiling planet'.

For politicians the war is a lesson in hubris for both sides. It is a theme of this book that both sides overreached. That is not to forgive the bestiality of Russian troops in Bucha and other places. Putin was clearly deluded about Ukraine's place in his vision of Greater Russia. But NATO gave good reason for Putin to be defensive.

Both sides need to learn from the lessons of this tragic and futile war. It will take generations to rebuild, including the damage caused by the 'cultural genocide': over a hundred important Ukrainian historical sites have been destroyed in the fighting or desecrated deliberately. Let's hope that humankind has the time before any other manmade climate catastrophes intrude.

For military historians much can be learnt from this nineteenth-century war fought with twentieth-century tactics and twenty-first century weaponry. Military staff colleges will no doubt indulge in many hours of exegesis. Both to wage and end, the 'cross-breed conflict' has discombobulated many of the finest military minds all over the planet.

An obvious historical analogy exists in the Spanish Civil War. Like NATO versus Russia, it was a local proxy war that led to a general war, the Second World War. Instead of studying the many arresting technical developments of the Russo-Ukrainian war, such as the extensive use of drones, a proper appreciation of the political failures would be more relevant. That is the best way to avoid the Third World War.

The usual analogy is the Cuban missile crisis of 1962 but the US national security was in play then in a way that it was not in the Ukraine war. They do, however, have some things in common. The most obvious similarity is that over sixty years later the West is faced yet again with a revanchist Russia testing the size of Washington's *cojones*.

As the great Russian pacifist Leo Tolstoy wrote:

In all history there is no war that was not hatched by governments, governments alone, independent of the interests of the people, for who war is always pernicious – even when successful.

Appendix 1

The Blame Game Again

I spoke to numerous experts about who to blame for the war. This is a short selection of the more interesting replies.

Moscow

As an example, on one side I asked Professor Vladimir Shubin, the Institute for African Studies, in Moscow. Vladimir I knew quite well because he had corrected so many mistakes that I had made about Russian military and intelligence matters in Africa. E-mail correspondence in March 2023.

1. Q. Was the West's failure to halt NATO expansion after German unification a major and justified cause of Russian hostility?
    A. I wouldn't use the word 'hostility'. Gorbachev had been cheated. The promises given him were false.
2. Q. After 1991 could the Russian Federation ever have established a close working relationship with NATO?
    A. The working relationship had already been established under Yeltsin and (Andrei) Kozyrev though many in Russia disapproved of this because the relationship counterposed Russia to the Global South. The relationship deteriorated after NATO attacked Yugoslavia.
3. Q. Were you surprised by the Russian army's poor performance in the first year of the Russo-Ukrainian war, especially considering the massive amount of re-organization and expenditure introduced by President Putin?

A. I would not call it 'poor performance', even if the 'special military operation' is taking a long time. The Russian army is facing an adversary trained, equipped (and sometimes even commanded) by dozens of other states. Fortunately, the Russian defence industry is successfully coping with Western weaponry.

4. Q. I believe that NATO is already (February 2023) at war with Russia. Do you agree?

A. It is true, though not in a legal sense. Now the armed conflict is not between Russia and Ukraine but between Russia and NATO on Ukrainian (and partly Russian) soil.

5. Q. It is my view that Russia will eventually 'win' in the Ukraine but at a very high cost to the Kremlin in blood and treasure. Do you agree?

A. No doubt but a higher cost is being paid by the people of Ukraine who are victims of the West's surrealistic hope to achieve Russia's 'strategic defeat'. Therefore Boris [Johnson] and Co. sabotaged the talks in Istanbul last year.

6. Q. Do you think China is more or less likely to attack Taiwan after considering the Russian experience in Ukraine?

A. It looks like they will hope to achieve a Hong Kong re-unification. However, they may take more radical steps if there are attempts to proclaim Taiwan's independence.

Senior British journalist in Ukraine

Lindsey Hilsum is the Channel Four News International Editor. I have had the privilege of working with her in a number of war zones over thirty years. She is one of the most hard-working and thoughtful of international correspondents. Correspondence in March 2023.

1. Q. Was the West's failure to stop NATO expansion after German re-unification a major and justified cause of Russian hostility?

A. No. Putin in his July 2021 essay makes it clear that this is a war of imperial re-conquest – his motivation is about reversing what he sees as the humiliation of the break-up of the Soviet Union, which was the end of the Russian Empire as created and expanded by Peter the Great and Catherine the Great. NATO is a secondary issue. The mistakes the West made, in my view, were three-fold: first orchestrating the collapse of the Russian economy and the wholesale privatization of the Russian state in the 1990s, breeding terrible deprivation and a new class of ultra-rich politically connected oligarchs. Second: becoming dependent on Russian energy and allowing western institutions, including banks, lawyers and estate agents, to make vast profits from Russian corruption. Third: failing to respond adequately to the annexation of Crimea and invasion of the Donbas. This made Putin think the West was corrupt and weak, and that he could invade Ukraine with few consequences.

2. Q. After 1991 could the Russian Federation ever have established a close working relationship with NATO?

A. Possibly if Yeltsin hadn't lost the plot, but it's unlikely as you still had hard-liners like [Yevgeny] Primakov in powerful positions. It's fair to say that western nations misjudged Russia and were too triumphalist about the collapse of the USSR, making it hard for Russian politicians to co-operate with NATO.

3. Q. Were you surprised by the Russian army's poor performance in the first year of the Russo-Ukrainian war especially considering the massive amount of re-organization and expenditure introduced by President Putin?

A. Yes, but others know more about this than I do. I was also surprised by the very good performance of the Ukrainians. In 2014 in Crimea, I watched Ukrainian forces lower their blue and yellow flag and leave their bases without firing a shot. They just surrendered, because they couldn't stand up to a bunch of little green men, who were really Russian Spetsnaz without insignia. Their performance in 2022 shows the impact of eight years of NATO training and equipment, as well as their high motivation.

4. Q. I believe NATO is already (in February 2023) at war with Russia. Do you agree?

   A. Not really. NATO is clearly doing a huge amount to protect Ukraine and the risks of escalation are great. But I don't buy the Russian narrative that this is a war between NATO and Russia, and that NATO caused this war. What was the alternative? Let Russia capture Kyiv and install a puppet government, so it could then threaten Poland and the Baltic States? Then NATO really would be at war with Russia. The distinction between helping Ukraine resist Russian occupation after an unprovoked invasion, and going to war with Russia may seem small but is politically crucial.

5. Q. It is my view that Russia will eventually 'win' in the Ukraine but at a very high cost to the Kremlin in blood and treasure. Do you agree?

   A. It is my view that journalists and military historians should not try to predict the future because they are usually wrong. If you look at previous recent Russian adventures – Georgia in 2008, Crimean/Donbas in 2014 – they tend to create frozen conflicts that impede independent states from joining Western institutions such as NATO or the EU, without those states reverting to the 'Ruski mir'. Look back further, and you have Finland which sacrificed Karelia in order to re-assert itself as a smaller but truly independent state. None of these are exact comparisons but may give some indication of alternative futures.

6. Q. Do you think China is more or less likely to attack Taiwan after considering the Russian experience in Ukraine?

   A. I think both China and Taiwan are studying this closely for lessons they can learn. Xi Jinping has given a date of 2027 for the potential re-incorporation of Taiwan into the PRC. I suspect a blockade of Taiwan might be more effective than an invasion. But as China apparently moves closer to Russia, and NATO countries continue to support Ukraine, all the pieces on the chessboard are in play.

Doing business in Russia

'David' is a multi-millionaire British businessman who has worked extensively in Russia. He did not want me to use his name. Interview on 23 February 2023.

RUSSIA HOLLOWED OUT AND BACKWARD
I first visited Russia about fifty years ago as a student. Later I went there professionally when working for large multinationals. I then started visiting regularly and frequently when I had my own gin company. I have probably been about thirty times over the last fifty years. Russia during the Soviet period was a pretty grim place. Russian cars, boats, trains and planes were all pretty dreadful. In the Ilyushins and Tupolev aircraft used by Aeroflot the seats, the seat belts and the toilets were awful. Some had no seat belts. The hotels were pretty dreadful too. Cumbersome and clunky and without any refinement. For the most part it worked (just about) but none of it was comfortable or pleasant. The restaurants were pretty pathetic too. In the 1980s and even 1990s when you travelled through the countryside you would see horses and carts and lots of people working the fields. When the Soviet copy of Concorde built by Tupolev crashed at the 1973 Paris Air Show, I was not surprised. In most of the fifty years I have known Russia the Russians have not had freedom of speech. My Western friends who have Russian wives and who live in Russia today tell me they cannot discuss the war or politics with their wives. Their wives accept the Kremlin narrative that the war in Ukraine was started by NATO.

CORRUPTION

You can only get import licences if you are a friend of a friend of Putin. My Western European importer told me one day that the Russian government had 'changed the rules' so that you could only obtain an import licence if you had the right connections. I have been a passenger in cars in Moscow or St Pete's [St Petersburg] when we would be stopped by a policeman who would say something like 'you were driving too fast' or 'your lights are not working properly' or 'you just drove through a red light'. My friend told me that this happens all the time. You give the policeman $20 or $30 dollars and he lets you off with a 'warning'.

On multiple occasions while staying in upmarket hotels a single woman would knock on my door in the evening asking if I wanted company. These women are told which doors to knock on by reception and no doubt the receptionist takes a cut of any money received. Many (most?) Russian businesses have someone who offers them 'protection'. My Western European friends confirmed to me that they had policemen on their payroll who could provide various services if required.

The Kremlin has the power of life or death over everyone. Just look at all the Russians who have been poisoned or who have mysteriously fallen out of upstairs windows. All around the world.

RUSSIA AND WAR SANCTIONS

My sense is that Putin will do everything to protect Moscow and St Pete's. It is the regions that will suffer most from the sanctions. I believe the sanctions are having an effect so that Russians are now buying more Chinese and Korean cars, for example.

RUSSIAN RESILIENCE

Look at how Russians just keep their mouths closed and get on with their lives. Look at how the street vendors in Moscow and St Pete's can stand outside all day at their tables selling a variety of goods. There can be snow on the ground and temperatures well below freezing. You would never see a similar scene in London, Paris or Berlin. But in Russia it is all perfectly normal. That said, many young Russians have fled to avoid military service. Perhaps they are displaying an alternative form of resilience.

HOW DO I SEE THE WAR ENDING

Needless to say, I do not know how the war will end. If forced to take a guess, I would say that the war will continue for a long time yet. Two, three or four years. The end will probably come with a negotiated settlement. Even the death of Putin, if that comes first, might not bring an end to the war. Zelensky has said he will not concede territory. Russia will almost certainly take the same stance.

I think we had better prepare for the long haul.

Appendix 2

Rebuilding Ukraine

Russia invaded so it should pay for reconstruction after the war ends. That is the most common view held in the West. But would it work?

In March 2023 the World Bank estimated that rebuilding Ukraine would cost at least $411 billion and the costs go up every day as Moscow keeps sending in missiles to destroy infrastructure.

One obvious answer is to use frozen Russian assets to put money into a pot to rebuild. Canada, for example, has passed legislation to allow frozen Russian assets to be deployed on behalf of Ukraine. In the USA members of Congress have introduced legislation to do the same. And EU members have considered doing the same at a recent summit, although the German chancellor, Otto Scholz, did say that such a course of action could violate international law.

Moral arguments support Ukraine as a victim of aggression and Russia could afford to finance reconstruction. And the West would benefit from a strong Ukrainian post-bellum economy that would be its best defence against further encroachments by its neighbour. And making Moscow pay could also deter military adventurism by other strongmen. Meanwhile, Western governments are broke after Covid and increased defence spending for NATO and Ukraine, let alone the green transition. Western electorates are showing signs of compassion fatigue with Ukraine and the side effects of the war, not least the energy hikes. So a common consensus is emerging: why should the West pay more for a war that it didn't start?

At the moment financial transfers from the US and EU amount to about $2.3 billion a month to Kyiv. To pay more than $411 billion, and climbing fast, on top of that is probably beyond the G7 governments, or rather the tolerance of their voters.

The governments of the USA, Australia, Canada, France, Germany, Italy, Japan, the UK and the European Commission seized about $300 billion in Russian central bank assets just after the invasion. That amounted to about half of Russian's foreign reserves at the time. Most of this money, about $200 billion, is frozen in European accounts. These governments have also confiscated tens of billions of dollars in assets belonging to Russian oligarchs and organizations.

So the c.$230-plus billion of frozen Russian funds in Europe could help fill the gap in funds for restoring Ukraine?

An opposing argument is that if central bank currency reserves are taken – 'garnished' is the technical term – then central banks will stop holding foreign reserves and the international financial system could become illiquid and even more unstable. But only central banks whose governments commit the most egregious violations of international norms, such as invading a neighbour, will be subject to such measures. Thus the risk will be severely limited to very bad boys (and girls) indeed. Others worry that if Washington and its allies grab Russian reserves then the dollar's role as an international currency could be severely tarnished. But this ignores the fact that there is no real alternative to the greenback. Beijing's yuan, despite all the fanfare, is nowhere near replacing the dollar as an international currency.

Would it be legal? So far, the lawyers have given no definitive answer.

Moscow had anticipated such action and so had moved many of its reserves. But if the remaining assets are taken this would provide a useful propaganda tool for Putin who always makes out that Russia is the victim of a Western conspiracy. Such a seizure would make peace, or armistice, negotiations more difficult. It could also encourage a much harder post-Putin line in the Kremlin. Offering the return of at least some of the frozen money could be a sweetener towards a deal that would then encourage good behaviour to get all the money back; in time, it might just help Moscow to adhere to any peace deals. Maybe.

Reparations have a bad history, however. Russians agreed to pay reparations to the Central Powers when Russia exited the war in the Treaty of Brest-Litovsk, which was repudiated by the Bolshevik government eight months later. A more obvious analogy is with the German reparations after the Great War. The war guilt clause of the Versailles Treaty assigned blame for the war to Germany. The massive reparations had devastating economic and political effects on the fragile Weimar democracy. Adolf Hitler used the reparations bill as a major plank in his propaganda. It is often argued that the war guilt cause and the massive sums demanded helped the rise of German militarism hell bent on revising the Versailles Treaty. It did a lot to help the aftermath of the Great War to become the Second World War.

Today's possibility of Russian 'war guilt' would be different. A reparations levy on Moscow would be a one-time event. It would not be a continuous sore as in inter-war Germany. Post-Putin leaders would not have the same incentive, as the Germans had, to mismanage their economy in order to wrest concessions from their creditors. There is no democracy in Russia to conserve now but the 'Versailles risk' is a central concern to the Western powers.

By the time the war ends, the real costs of rebuilding Ukraine could be over a trillion dollars. If the first year of the war cost $411 billion then that is more than double the size of the pre-invasion economy. Kyiv says it needs an immediate $14 billion to fund critical infrastructure in 2023 alone. Ukraine has outlined some of its urgent needs in housing, health, transport infrastructure and agriculture. In the next ten years the Ukrainian government says it needs, for example, $38 billion for 'explosive hazard management'.

Early in 2023 the US government used $5 million from Russian oligarch seizures to be sent to Ukraine. The Treasury Secretary, Janet Yellen, has said that 'significant legal obstacles' stand in the way of confiscating and then transferring frozen Russian assets. A bi-partisan group of US lawyers has introduced legislation to give the president the legal authority to do so. There are precedents: Ronald Reagan and George H.W. Bush did seize Iranian government assets in 1981 and Iraqi funds in 1992 respectively.

EU leaders are considering how to use billions of dollars accrued in interest to be transferred into an EU national investment fund. The

EU has talked of a new 'Marshall Plan' for Ukraine and has worked on practical measures at Ukraine Recovery Conferences. So far, the European Commission has provided 15 billion euro for financial, humanitarian, and military support. Brussels set up what it called 'The Ukraine Facility' that will provide predictable financial support for 2024–27. One of the specific programmes is the 100 million euro for Ukrainian schools. Part of that money is being spent on school buses to transport the children safely.

In June 2023 another Ukraine Recovery Conference was held in London. The war has made Ukraine the world's biggest building site and could be ripe for investment as well as aid, if the war can end. Investors such as BlackRock and JP Morgan Chase are working with Kyiv on a development plan. The official slogan is that 'Reconstruction is already happening. It's part of our resistance'. One Ukrainian minster, Oleksandra Azarkhina, said at the London conference: 'Ukraine needs help – not just on the battlefield but in terms of private and public investment.'

Ursula von der Leyen, the European Commission President, led the way with reconstruction efforts. But selfishness intrudes as well: Ukraine is the biggest country by area that lies entirely in Europe. And it has twenty-one of the critical thirty raw materials needed by the EU. Ukraine also has the largest underground storage facilities for gas in Europe.

Ukraine has to be rebuilt but it also has to sort its corruption if it can hope to join the EU in perhaps twenty years. So, Brussels will control the money carefully to avoid Ukraine's chronic bad financial habits. Ukrainian ministers try to point out most of Ukraine is not occupied and is not in Russia's crosshairs. After this was said in London, Moscow sent a barrage of drones and missiles to attack Lvov near the Polish border. There won't be much work done on the gigantic building site until Putin stops or is stopped.

Seventy years after the US-led Marshall Plan saved Europe the question of rebuilding a war-ravaged part of Europe has returned. And the scope of the challenge keeps shifting with the war. The destruction of the Nova Kakhovka Dam unleashed massive environmental as well as structural damage, let alone all the houses destroyed. Besides dams, over 300-plus bridges have to be rebuilt as well as the millions of tons of rubble removed.

Europe and America are providing lots of promised goodies and offering money and goodwill. But it all depends on the war ending. As long as Putin sits on his throne in the Kremlin the war will go on and no talk of war crimes or reparation are likely. Of course, Putin might just slip up and land in an ICC member country and get arrested. That is highly unlikely for the super-cautious Russian president. Unless, however, major rebuilding of the economic and social structure begins soon, the bitterness in Ukraine will fester as it did with the Holodomor of the 1930s. Nobody in the European borderlands can move on unless peace and reconstruction begin in earnest.

Appendix 3

NATO's Expansion

How and why the alliance was expanded

The important enlargements took place in the post-Berlin Wall 1990s when President Bill Clinton came to believe that it was in the American interest to have the 'broadest, deepest alliance' possible. When Poland joined in 1999 the alliance gained a border with Russia, the Kaliningrad enclave, and that opened the door to many future members. When Estonia joined in 2004 NATO's border moved again to less than 100 miles from Putin's hometown of St Petersburg. In 1989 the distance from the Russian border had been 1,200 miles.

The NATO expansion assured the countries freed from the Soviet yoke. But now the post-Cold War order was starting to look like the original Cold War except that the border lines had been moved far to the east. But did it have to be this way? Could Moscow have been brought in from the cold? Could the process have stopped with the re-unification of Germany, a country at the epicentre of the Second World War and the Cold War? When President George H.W. Bush was asked about compromise with Moscow by curbing NATO's growth, he said, 'To hell with that.' NATO had been the backbone of Western and, especially, Washington's success since 1949. So why change it? was the dominant motif of most, though not all, foreign policy wonks in the American capital.

The American president persuaded Chancellor Helmut Kohl to pay the massive bill for unification. Meanwhile Washington finessed the Russians by implying that as Moscow had allowed Germans to unify then Washington did not need to advance NATO further. It was also debated whether President Gorbachev should be encouraged to keep a sort of Warsaw Pact as a fig-leaf.

Suddenly Pandora's box was opened up for Washington. The 1991 coup in Moscow and then the very unexpected collapse of the Soviet Union, ushered in many uncertainties, especially about all the 'loose nukes' in Russia and in some of the successor states. The political mayhem also allowed a new flexibility America had not enjoyed since 1945. But Washington was distracted, not least by the First Gulf War, and did not grasp the opportunity to pull Moscow into a friendlier embrace. Some debt forgiveness and stronger connection with, and attention from, NATO may have helped. Soon hyper-inflation and corruption in the Russian economy was undermining the tender shoots of democracy. His heart condition and excess alcohol contributed to Boris Yeltsin's increasingly erratic behaviour. And the presence of anti-Western extremists in the Duma under a weak Yeltsin leadership added to the sense of turmoil. Naturally, the newly freed eastern Europe states were queueing up to be allowed to join NATO and the EU. Polish pleas for freedom had been ignored in the post-war late 1940s. After all, the West had technically gone to war in 1939 because of the German invasion of Poland. This time Washington did not want to be seen to ignore Poland and other eastern European countries – and many politicians in Washington had large émigré communities, not least the Poles, in their constituencies.

Bill Clinton did try to maintain co-operation with Moscow as the former Warsaw Pact satellites started to jump ship. The fundamental question was: would Washington go to war for all these millions of new Europeans who wanted to be defended under Article 5? The old Charles de Gaulle question (would the US government sacrifice Washington for Paris?) was asked again and again. The USA tried to develop an incremental partnership strategy that expected the new states to earn their Article 5 protection. The man who played a key part in this was the chairman of the Joint Chiefs of Staff, the Polish-born General John Shalikashvili; he was appointed by Clinton in 1993. The general was the first foreign-born man to become chairman.[1] The soldier was an able diplomat, not least with the Partnership for Peace that included ex-Soviet states and with some Russian acceptance. Washington and Moscow co-operated on some aspects of the crisis in Bosnia meanwhile.

Yeltsin's use of violence against his opponents in Moscow and especially the savagery in Chechnya and the revival of hard-line old-style nationalists and communists in Russia helped to reinforce the pressure on Clinton to accept full-fledged new NATO members. On the other hand, in 1999 Moscow was very alarmed at NATO's direct involvement in the Balkans, especially over Kosovo. NATO appeared to be very aggressive. Moscow's foreign policy elites then began to conclude that the Partnership for Peace had a been a ruse to fool them all along when in fact Washington was very reluctant to suck in new members all expecting the shield of Article 5. There was no long-term plan let alone a conspiracy – Clinton did not know where to draw the line, literally, of pro-Western and pro-Russian states.

Clinton had not given up on greater co-operation with Moscow but the big differences over the civil wars in Yugoslavia, Moscow's support for Belgrade, and flashpoints such as the Russian armoured dash for Pristina airport in 1999 tended to cause more frictions in Moscow-Washington relations. Nevertheless, experts in the State Department did warn the president about the dangers of further humiliating Moscow with continuing NATO enlargement as well as undermining existing arms controls. Expansion was now the accepted norm but how far?

In 1999 Washington decided to welcome the Baltic states. Technically, the USA had never accepted the loss of their sovereignty by the Soviet occupation at the end of the Second World War. That decision and the elevation of President Putin in the same year meant that a new iron curtain of sorts was descending. Countries such as Ukraine and Georgia and, perhaps, also Belarus ended up in the grey zone they had been trying to avoid. So, 1999 had rubbished all the liberal hopes of a decade before that history was ending as states reverted to liberal democracy. In Russia's case 'revert' was an odd word: it had enjoyed only very brief periods of what the West would recognize as liberal democracy. Gorbachev had to tried to reform but he ended up scorned by most of his fellow Russians; but it was in the longer term a heroic failure. Yeltsin had tried to democratize Russia; he was also well-meaning in his own muddled way – instead he passed the baton to another Stalin.

Given that Russia, once it sorted out its domestic chaos, would once more end up as a big player, and still flaunting the world's biggest nuclear arsenal, should more have been done to include Russia in the European security architecture? Possibly, but morally the newly freed states of Europe also had the right to choose NATO and the EU. Perhaps some of Putin's unceasingly authoritarian methods, for example in the second war in Chechnya, were choices he made – they were not foisted on him by Washington. As it happens, the USA *supported* – on the sidelines – some of the tough measures against revived Islamism. And Moscow even helped with bases to deploy US forces against Al-Qaeda.

If some critics have said NATO was too quick to expand, then they also say that the EU was too slow. The EU had less influence in the democratization process and economic reforms than many ex-Soviet states put into joining the security alliance. The 'big-bang' expansion of NATO in 2004 was bound to cause genuine anxiety and anger in Moscow. Finland and Sweden had talked about including the Baltics in a separate Nordic pact. It was not to be and the final nails in the coffin, as far as Moscow was concerned, was Finland and Sweden finally abandoning their decades of neutrality and joining up because of the Russo-Ukrainian war.

Clinton had shown caution but President George H.W. Bush's son, George W. Bush, did the opposite. As one prominent expert on the NATO expansion put it, 'He took the keys of the NATO car and gunned it down the open road.'[2] The younger Bush attended a NATO summit in Latvia, the first such event in former Soviet territory and then at the Bucharest summit in 2008 he pushed hard for the inclusion of Georgia and Ukraine. President Putin took all this very badly. The Bucharest summit came on top of America's invasion of Iraq in 2003 and the 2007 decision to erect ballistic missile defences in the form of ten ground-based interceptors in Poland and a radar facility in the Czech Republic. All this happening around the time of the colour revolutions proved to be Putin's breaking point.

Moscow now beefed up its armed forces and started interfering in Georgia and later in Ukraine, knowing the Alliance would not accept the membership of a country already involved in conflict. So NATO suspended the NATO Russia Council, set up in May 2002.

Was expansion a bad idea? Obviously 'yes' if the answer is coming from Moscow but 'thank God' from Vilnius or Warsaw. Moscow has indulged in various forms of subversion in Europe and North America but it has not invaded a new NATO member. Article 5 has been invoked but to fight Jihadists after 9/11. Far from being 'brain dead', it could be argued that NATO has expanded itself into necessity again, despite Donald Trump's embrace of Putin, not least since the invasion of Ukraine.

Appendix 4

How Likely is the Chance of the Ukraine-Russian War Going Nuclear?

Kicking off a nuclear conflict?

Serhii Plokhy is a Harvard professor of Ukrainian extraction who has been quoted a number of times in this book. He has just published an excellent book on The Cuban Missile Crisis (*Nuclear Folly*); what is important is that he has read the recently de-classified KGB files and he also thinks that a nuclear war is possible. I agree with him, hence this short appendix.

Plokhy concludes his book with this comment:

John Kennedy and Nikita Khruschev managed to avoid nuclear war after making almost every mistake conceivable and every step imaginable to cause it. But they did not step into the traps so masterfully created by themselves because they did not believe they could win a nuclear war, nor were they prepared to pay a price for such a victory. It is hard to imagine what the outcome of the Cuban crisis might have been if the two leaders had a more cavalier attitude toward the nuclear arms.

Kennedy was soon assassinated and not long afterwards Khrushchev was sacked by his politburo for his 'nuclear adventurism'. The near Armageddon soon led to elaborate arms control agreements and hotlines so that the two nuclear superpowers could talk and avoid the possibility of war by accident.

Now it is far more dangerous because nearly all the agreements have expired, especially the Russian and American withdrawal from the

Intermediate Range Nuclear Forces Treaty negotiated by Reagan and Gorbachev in 1987. It is so alarming to be without these treaties because a big war has broken out in Europe again.

Many other states have developed open or covert nuclear weapons programmes and some, like Iran, have threatened to use them, against Israel. Also, nuclear weapons are now often smaller and more accurate, not least with the s-called MIRVs – Multiple Independently Targeted Re-entry Vehicles.

Moscow is once again a revisionist power even though it has ditched its communist ideology. Washington espouses a philosophy that is opposed to the authoritarian states of Russia (and China). Cultural differences persist between the old superpower rivals that can inspire all sorts of misunderstandings about military intentions. Above all, Moscow has good reason to be concerned that America's new precise weapons and their locations in Eastern Europe could possibly permit a successful first strike, thus blowing up the whole Mutual Assured Destruction military balance of the Cold War. It is surely sensible to worry about the sanity let alone the need for political skills and leadership, in both Washington and Moscow. On top of that, cyber-attacks could take control of a rival's nuclear arsenal without firing a shot. In theory. And increasingly in practice. There hangs the plot of another Terminator film.

Putin has been in control of his arsenal but the Wagner mutiny suggests that some of the Russian intelligence and military elite went rogue. And Joe Biden often raises questions about whether dementia could get the better of him in another Cuban missile style crisis. Putin and his acolytes have seriously sabre-rattled the use of tactical nuclear devices, including for demonstration effect in Ukraine but offshore from Britain and France as well creating tsunamis off the US coasts. Worse, some of the media in Russia have indicated that a tactical nuclear war is no longer unthinkable.

With so many drivers towards a nuclear holocaust, no wonder the Doomsday Clock is 1.5 minutes to midnight. The writers and editors on the *Bulletin of Atomic Scientists* know more than most.

The most pressing concern is ending the war in Ukraine before it gets out of hand, not least by a nuclear accident, let alone actually deliberately firing a so-called tactical nuclear weapon. Or two. If it lands on your head, or your city, it is not tactical. It is strategic mass murder. The peace treaty which ends the war in Ukraine must also lead quickly to new arms control arrangements. Above all, the citizens of the West, who sometimes can influence their governments, need to relearn the lessons of the past. Today social media can replace marches and ban the bomb posters. And it is to be hoped that we all have more than ninety seconds to do all this.

Notes

Chapter 1: Are Russians different?
1. Sheila Fitzpatrick, *The Shortest History of the Soviet Union* (Old Street Publishing, Exeter, 2023) p.53.
2. Mark Galeotti, 'Can Art Get a Grip on Putin?' *Sunday Times Magazine*, 18 June 2023.

Chapter 2: Understanding Russia
1. At Pristina Airport, I spoke to rather bedraggled Russians who showed me inside their armoured vehicles – they looked like museum pieces. In the rush they had not had time to bring much spare clothing. They chatted in their dirty vests while some of the uniforms were drying on a makeshift line hanging between their vehicles and nearby trees.
2. Medea Benjamin and Nicolas J.S. Davies, *War in Ukraine: Making Sense of a Senseless Conflict* (OR Books, London, 2022) pp. 18–19.
3. His father had been a Red Army general and his mother was Jewish, a typical example of the country of mixed heritage especially amid the neo-Nazi accusations by the Kremlin. Vitali Klitschko became Mayor of Kyiv and a stout defender of the country during the Russo-Ukrainian war.
4. *Strategic Survey 2014* (IISS, London, 2014) p.160.

Chapter 3: A Man Called Volodymyr
1. Serhii Rudenko, *Zelensky: A Biography* (Polity, Cambridge, 2022) p.194.
2. Ibid., p.164.

Chapter 4: A Man Called Vladimir
1. For details of the Dresden period see Catherine Belton, *Putin's People: How the KGB Took Back Russia and then Took on the West* (William Collins, London, 2021) pp.19–50.
2. For more details, see Paul Moorcraft, *Dying For the Truth: The Concise History of Frontline War Reporting* (Pen and Sword, Barnsley, 2017) p.179.
3. To quote an example from the author's own experience. During a heavy Soviet offensive around Kabul in mid-1984, I saw a number of examples of where Russian attack helicopters and aircraft had cornered a large number of Mujahedin but they followed strict protocols and never took advantage of targets of opportunity, even before US Stingers were introduced to the battlefield.
4. en.kremlin.ru/d/66181. 12 July 2021

Chapter 5: Putin's Wars
1. Mark Galeotti, *Putin's Wars: From Chechnya to Ukraine* (Osprey, Oxford, 2022). p.203.
2. Robert Kagan, 'Putin Makes His Move', *Washington Post*, 11 August 2008.
3. For a detailed analysis of the war against Islamic State, see Paul Moorcraft, *The Jihadist Threat* (Pen and Sword, Barnsley, 2017).

Chapter 6: The Blame Game
1. Rodric Braithwaite, *Russia: Myths and Realities* (Profile, London, 2022) p.234.
2. 'Why the Ukraine Crisis is the West's Fault', *Foreign Affairs*, (September/October 2014).

Chapter 8: The Russian Invasion of Ukraine
1. Philip Short, *Putin: His Life and Times* (Bodley Head, London, 2022) p.656.
2. Serhii Plokhy, *The Russo-Ukrainian War* (Penguin, London, 2023) p.155.

Chapter 9: The Wagner Mutiny
1. A pattern emerged: in Sudan the militia rose up against the regular army. This resulted in a bitter civil war. In Russia the Wagner Group stopped short of advancing on Moscow.
2. The Germans also used penal battalions.

Chapter 11: Information warfare and propaganda
1. 'The Russian Firehose of Falsehood Propaganda', the Rand Corporation https://www.rand.org/pubs/perspectives/PE198.html
2. Lisa Haseldine, 'Textbook warfare', the *Spectator*, 19 August 2023.
3. Rosie Kinchen, 'Last Man in Moscow', *Sunday Times Magazine*, 16 July 2023.

Chapter 12: Give Peace a Chance
1. Medea Benjamin and Nicolas J.S. Davies, *War in Ukraine: Making Sense of a Senseless Conflict (*OR Books, 2022) p.179
2. The author met him on a number of occasions in London.
3. Kim Willsher, '"Shameful" Nicolas Sarkozy under fire or defending Putin', *The Guardian*, 19 August 2023.

Chapter 13: Give War a Chance
1. Lawrence Freedman, *Command: The Politics of Military Operation from Korea to Ukraine* (Allen Lane, London, 2022) p.399.
2. Mark Galeotti, *Putin's Wars: From Chechnya to Ukraine* (Osprey, Oxford, 2022) p.350.
3. George Grylls, 'Suicide squad on front line clearing Putin's landmines', *The Times*, 10 August 2023.

Chapter 14: A New Era?
1. Serhii Plokhy, *The Russo-Ukrainian War* (Penguin, London, 2023) p.293.

Appendix 3: NATO: How and why the alliance was expanded

1. General John Shalikashvili was the scion of a Georgian noble family. His father, Prince Dmitri, served in the Imperial Russian army. After the Bolshevik revolution Dmitri became a lieutenant colonel in the army of the independent republic of Georgia. When the Soviet Union invaded, Prince Dimitri was abroad and then took up refuge with other Georgian exiles in Poland. The chairman's father met and married a part-German-part-Polish woman, also a part of a noble Russian family. In 1939 the elder Shalikashvili fought with the Poles against the German invasion. In 1941 he enlisted in the Georgian Legion which was recruited to fight the USSR; it later became a part of the Georgian Waffen SS and Shalikashvili *père* was captured fighting in Normandy. The young son, John, fled from Poland in the closing days of the Second World War and lived in Germany until young John was 16 when his family emigrated to Peoria, Illinois. It must have run in the blood because he had a stellar career in the army, especially in Iraq. With Shalikashvili's amazing mix of European heritage and languages, Clinton chose a very suitable Mr Fix-It for NATO expansion.
2. M.E. Sarotte, *Not One Inch: America, Russia and the Making of the Post–Cold War Stalemate* (Yale, New Haven, 2021) p.348.

Select Bibliography (in English)

Abelow, Benjamin, *How the West Brought War to Ukraine* (Siland Press, Barrington, Massachusetts, 2022).
Applebaum, Anne, *Red Famine: Stalin's War on Ukraine* (Penguin, London, 2018).
Ash, Timothy Garton, *Homelands: A Personal History of Europe* (Bodley Head, London, 2023).
Beevor, Antony, *Russia: Revolution and Civil War 1917–1921*, (Weidenfeld and Nicolson, London, 2022).
——, *Stalingrad* (Penguin, London, 2007).
Belton, Catherine, *Putin's People* (William Collins, London, 2020).
Benjamin, Medea and Nicolas J.S. Davies, *War in Ukraine: Making Sense of a Senseless Conflict* (OR Books, London, 2022).
Braithwaite, Roderic, *Russia: Myths and Realities* (Profile, London, 2022).
Browder, Bill, *Freezing Order* (Simon and Schuster, London, 2022).
Bullough, Oliver, *Butler to the World: How Britain became the Servant of Tycoons, Tax Dodgers, Kleptocrats and Criminals* (Profile, London, 2002).
Conquest, Robert, *The Harvest of Sorrow: Soviet Collectivisation and the Terror-Famine* (Bodley Head, London, 2018).
Figes, Orlando, *The History of Russia* (Bloomsbury, London, 2022).
Fitzpatrick, Sheila, *The Shortest History of the Soviet Union* (Old Street Publishing, Exeter, 2023).
Freedman, Lawrence, *Command: The Politics of Military Operations from Korea to Ukraine* (Allen Lane, London, 2022).
Galeotti, Mark, *Putin's Wars: From Chechnya to Ukraine* (Osprey, Oxford, 2022).
Hess, Maximilian, *Economic War and the Global Conflict between Russia and the West* (Hurst, London, 2023).
Kuzio, Taras, *Putin's War against Ukraine* (University of Toronto, Toronto, 2017).
Montefiore, Simon Sebag, *Stalin: The Court of the Red Tsar* (Weidenfeld and Nicolson, London, 2020).
Moorcraft, Paul, *The Jihadist Threat: Re-conquest of the West?* (Pen and Sword, Barnsley, 2015).
——, *Dying for the Truth: The Concise History of Frontline War Reporting* (Pen and Sword, Barnsley, 2016).
——, *Superpowers, Rogue States and Terrorism: Countering Security Threats to the West* (Pen ad Sword, Barnsley, 2017).
——, *North Korea: Warring with the World* (Pen and Sword, Barnsley, 2021).
Nestor, William, *Putin's Virtual War* (Pen and Sword, Barnsley, 2019).
Owen, David, *Riddle, Mystery and enigma: Two Hundred Years of British-Russian Relations* (Haus, London, 2021).

Plokhy, Serhii, *Nuclear Folly: A New History of the Cuban Missile Crisis* (Allen Lane, London, 2021).
——, *The Russo-Ukrainian War* (Allen Lane, London, 2023).
Rudenko, Serhii, *Zelensky: A Biography* (Polity, Cambridge, UK, 2022).
Sarotte, M.E., *Not One Inch: America, Russia and the Making of the Post-Cold War Stalemate* (Yale, New Haven, 2021).
Shishkin, Michael, *My Russia: War or Peace?* (Riverrun, London, 2023).
Short, Philip, *Putin: His Life and Times* (Bodley Head, London, 2022).
Smith, Michael, *The Special Relationship: The True Story of how the British and US Secret Services work Together* (Simon and Schuster, London, 2022).
Stallard, Katie, *Dancing on Bones: History and Power in China, Russia and North Korea* (Oxford University Press, Oxford, 2022).
Weiner, Tim, *The Folly and the Glory: America, Russia and Political Warfare, 1945–2020* (Henry Holt, New York, 2020).

Index

Abramovich, Roman, 119, 150
Airbus, 103
Al-Assad, Bashar, 13, 15, 72
Al-Bashir, Omar, 106
Al-Qaeda, xxix, 115, 172
Apartheid, 1
Apple, 103
Armata tank, 12
Armenia, 60–1
Ashdown, Paddy, 149
Austin, Lloyd, 31, 119
Avakov, Arsen, 30
Azerbaijan, 60–1
Azov Battalion (Regiment), 23, 31, 87

Bakanov, Ivan, 28, 30
Baker, James, 66
Baltic states, 73–6
BBC, 98, 128
Belarus, joint military exercises with Russia, 79
Bennett, Naftali, 119
Berezovsky, Boris, 10
Beslan school siege, 38, 51
Biden, Joe, 20, 31–2, 45, 81, 118, 145
  alleged dementia, 175
Boeing, 103
Bolsheviks, 6, 48
Bowen, Jeremy, 52–3
Braithwaite, Rodric, 62
Brezhnev, Leonid, 64
BRICS, 44, 145, 152
Brown Moses (Eliot Higgins), 113
Bucha atrocities, 83, 85, 109
Budapest Memorandum, 20, 73
Bulletin of Atomic Scientists, xxix, 46
Burns, William J., 66

Bush, George H.W., 166, 169
Bush, George W., 56, 172
Byzantium, 2

Cameron, David, 58
Cardiff Philharmonic Orchestra, 102
Catherine the Great, 7
Ceausesçu, Nicolai, 8, 48
Chechnya, 11, 36–7, 49–55
Chernobyl, 3, 81–2, 85–6, 114, 130, 132
Chernomyrdin, Viktor, 36
China, possible war with, 146–7
Chinese embassy, Belgrade, attacked by NATO, 62
Chomsky, Noam, 118
CIA, 32, 78, 135
Clark, Wesley, 11
Clinton, Bill, 131, 169–71
Clinton, Hillary, 72
CNN, 128
Cold War (First), 4
Collective Security Treaty Organization, 60, 147
CPOA (nuclear deal with Iran) 16
Crimea, 1
  return to Russia, 13
  autonomous republic, 16
  invasion, 22
Cross-breed conflict, xxxi
Cuban missile crisis, xxviii, xxxi, 68, 155, 174
Cyber warfare, 141–2

Dagestan, 50
da Silva, Luiz Lula, 121
de Gaulle, Charles, 75–6

Donetsk People's Republic, 22, 26, 80
    annexation, 88
Dozhd, 110
Dr Strangelove, 75
Dubrovka Theatre attack, 37, 51
Dugin, Alexsandr, 4–5
Dugina, Darya, 5

Ekaterinburg SSN, 42
Ekho Moscovy, 110
Erdoğan, Recep, 59–60, 119
Eurasian Economic Union, 10
Euromaidan, 19–21
European Union,
    no war among members, xxx
    reluctance to let Ukraine join, 18
    reconstructions of Ukraine, 152, 165–7

Falkland Islanders, 10
Fedorov, Mikhailo, 143
Fitzpatrick, Sheila, 2
Ford, Robert, 59
Foundation of Geopolitics, 5
Freedman, Lawrence, 125
FSB, 36–7, 40, 95–8, 100

Gaddafi, Muamar, 14
Galeotti, Mark, 4, 57–8
Gazprom, 21
GCHQ, xxviii
Georgia, 55–7
Gerasimov, Valery, 93–101, 135
Ghost of Kyiv, 109
Gorbachev, Mikhail, 64–6, 103, 157, 169, 171, 175
    wanted to save USSR, 3
    return of Crimea, 13
Groysman, Vlodymyr, 29
GRU, 100
Guterres, António, 119

Hezbollah, 59
Hilsum, Lindsey, 158–9
Hitler, Adolf, xxix, 9, 54, 56, 136, 154, 166
Holodomor, 168

Human Rights Watch, 85
Hussein, Saddam, 53
Hybrid war, xxviii, xxxi, 10, 14

Ilves, Toomas, 124
IMF, 152
Intermediate Range Nuclear Forces Treaty, 175
International Atomic Energy Agency, 86–7
International Criminal Court, 63, 106, 145, 152
International Institute of Strategic Studies, 24
International Maritime Organization, 129
Iranian Revolutionary Guard, 59
Islamic State, 9, 154
Israel, building settlements, 108

Jackson, Mike, 12
Johnson, Boris, 76, 100–101, 119, 158

Kabaeva, Alina, 46–7
Kadyrov, Ramzan, 51, 53–4, 83, 136
Kagan, Robert, 56
Kahn, Herman, 131
Kennan, George, 68
Kennedy, John F., xxxii, 174
KGB, 35
    and Romania, 48
    HQ in Vilnius, 74
Khodorkovsky, Mikhail, xiii, 38, 98
Khrushchev, Nikita, xxxii
    donation of Crimea, 14, 174
Kim Jong-un, 75, 148
Kissinger, Henry, 75, 120, 131, 147
Kiyashko, Olena, 32–3
Klitschko, Vitali, 19–20, 82
Kohl, Helmut, 169
Kolomoyskyi, Ihor, 29
Kosovo, 11, 14, 56, 62, 64, 146, 171
Kozyrev, Andrei, 4, 157
Kuchma, Leonid, 16, 30
Kuleba, Dmytro, 121
Kurds, 58
Kursk, sinking, 37

Kuwait, babies taken from incubators, 109
Kvartal 95, 27–8, 30, 33

Lavrov, Sergey, 68, 119, 121, 145, 147
League of Nations, 105
Lenin, Vladimir, 7
Little Green Men, 11, 21, 114, 160
Litvinenko, Alexander, xiv–xv, xix, 6, 51
Lockheed Martin, 67
Loyn, David, 50
Luhansk People's Republic, 22–3, 26, 80
 annexation, 88
Lukashenko, Alexander, 83, 97, 147

Mabetex, 37
Macron, Emmanuel, 29, 87, 145, 150
Malaysian Airlines Flight MH17, 11, 70, 73, 114
Maskhadov, Aslan, 50
Maskirovka, 10
McCain, John, 91
McDonalds, 103
Mearsheimer, John, 66
Membership Action Plan, 56
Merkel, Angela, 39
Meta, 109
Milley, Mark, 120–1
Milošević, Slobodan, xxxii
Ministry of Defence, UK, 80, 88
Minsk Accords, 26, 71
Moldova, 49–50
Molotov-Ribbentrop accord, 49
Mongol yoke, xxx, 2
Morenets, Svitlana, 139
Mosaic war, 144
Moskva, sinking, 129
Munich Security Conference, 32, 39
Muratov, Dmitry, 130
Musk, Elon, 82–3, 120, 143–4

Nagorno-Karabakh, 26, 49, 60
National Endowment for Democracy, 20
National Security Agency (US), 142
National Security Council (Russia), 80
NATO,
 a capitalistic tool, 13
 western threat 14
 crimes against Moscow, 15
 aggressive alliance, 64–5
 bad interventions, 146
 expansion, 169–73
Navalny, Alexei, xvii–xviii, xix–xx, 25–6, 101, 110, 146, 154
Nehammer, Karl, 119
New START Treaty, 132
Nixon, Richard, 64, 75, 147
NKVD, 34
Nord Stream 2, 104
Normandy Format, 31
Northern Fleet, 3
Novaya Gazeta, 4, 38, 52, 80, 130
Nuclear weapons, Russian doctrine, xxix, 174–7

Obama, Barack, xvi, 12, 15, 24, 58–9, 132, 141
'Odesa Massacre', 22
Oligarchs, 6
Operation DESERT STORM, 76
Operation IRAQI FREEDOM, 57
Operation LENTIL, 50
Operation OLYMPIC GAMES, 141
Operation OVERLORD, 76
Operation SEA BREEZE, 67
Orange Revolution, 15, 17–19
Ostalgie, xxxi

Pandora Papers, 28
Patriarch Kirill, 44, 138
Patrushev, Nikolai, 135, 153
Peace deals, 118–24
Peace Research Institute, 138
Pentagon, 69, 82, 100, 138
Perestroika, 49
Pilger, John, 51
Plokhy, Serhii, 145–7, 174
Politkovskaya, Anna, 38–9, 52
Pope, the, 121
Poroshenko, Petro, 23, 29
Prigozhin, Yevgeny, 4, 91–101, 151
Primakov, Yevgeny, xii, 159
Propaganda, 107–17
Putin, Spiridon, 34
Putin, Vladimir,

self-image, xxviii
survival, xxxii
and Alexsandr Dugin, 4
lack of ideology, 10
high poll ratings, 14, 25
an actor, 33
career, 34–47
work in KGB, 35
reform of armed forces, 41–2
his writings, 44
his wars, 48–61
invasion of Ukraine, 79–90
and Wagner Group, 91–101
possible peace deals, 122
threat to use nukes, 131
Rambo image, 134
legacy, 153
Pyatt, Geoffrey R., 20

Qin Gang, 123
Queen Elizabeth, HMS, sinking, 77

Radio Free Europe/Liberty, 112
Ramaphosa, Cyril, 122
Rasmussen, Anders, 122
Rasmussen, Lars, 122
Reagan, Ronald, 29, 64, 166, 175
Reparations, 165–8
Reznikov, Oleksii, 122
Right Sector, 20, 22–3
Rosenberg, Steve, 115–16
Royal Military Academy, Sandhurst, xxv, 8
RT, 109, 112–14
Rubley, Andrey, 102
Russia,
    deal with NATO, xxii
    humbling after end of USSR, xxix
    geography, 1
Russians, paranoid, 1

Saakashvili, Mikheil, 56–7
Sanctions, 102–106, 162
Sarkozy, Nicolas, 55, 124
Sawyers, John, 72
SBU, 28
Schama, Simon, 148

Schröder, Gerhard, 47
Second World War, xxx, 1, 8, 10, 16, 20, 43, 46, 50, 79, 94, 125, 150, 155, 166, 169, 171
Secret Intelligence Service (MI6), xxvii, 72, 79
Servant of the People, 28–30
Sevastopol, 11, 16, 22, 48, 56, 128–9, 144
Shalikashvili, John, 170–1
Shefir, Serhiy, 31
Shevardnadze, Eduard, 56
Shirreff, Richard, 76–8
Shishkin, Mikhail, 5–6
Shkrebneva, Lyudmila, 46
Shoigu, Sergei, 93–101, 119, 135
Short, Philip, 110
Shubin, Vladimir, xxvi, 157–8
Siloviki, 5, 154
Skripal, Sergei, xix, 6
Skripal, Yulia, xix, 6
Smith, Vaughan, 50
Snake Island, 82, 87, 109, 116, 129
Snowden, Edward, xviii, 142
Soche Winter Olympics, 43
Somoilenko, Illia, 87
SpaceX, 143
Spiritual values, 3
Stalin, Joseph, xxiii, 3, 5, 8–10, 34, 45, 50, 56, 93, 125, 153–4, 171
Starlink, 83, 142–4
Stavridis, James, 77
Stefanchuk, Ruslan, 81
Stoltenberg, Jens, 83
Stuxnet, 141
Sudan, 82
Surovikin, Sergey, 95–6, 99
Svoboda Party, 19–21
SWIFT system, 102
Syria, xix, xxxi, 9, 12–13, 16, 33, 45, 58–60, 84, 92, 95, 97, 113
Syrsky, Oleksandr, 82

Tolstoy, Leo, 2, 102, 156
Transnistria, 26, 33, 39, 48–9, 87
Transparency International Corruption Perceptions Index, 134
Treaty of Brest-Litovsk, 8, 165

Treaty of Versailles, 166
Trump, Donald, xx, 31, 45, 59, 64, 72, 75–6, 131–2, 173
Tymoshenko, Yulia, 18–19

Ukraine,
  independence, 63
  Russian invasion, 79–90
Ukrainian Insurgent Army, 20
Ukrainian nationalists, 16
United Russia Party, xiii, xv–xvii, xix, 26, 40
Unity Party, 36
USSR,
  isolation from the West, 2
  competition with the West, 3
  collapse, 3, 62, 170
  Russians abroad, 48
Utkin, Dimitry, 100

Vershbow, Alexander, 25
Vigor, Peter, 8
VKontakte, 112
Von der Leyen, Ursula, 167
Vozhd, 5

Wagner Group, 59, 88–9, 91–101, 136, 114, 116, 136, 138, 146, 153–4, 175
Wallace, Ben, 80
Warsaw Pact, xxviii, 8, 65, 169–70

Wick, John, 6
World Bank, 164
World Jewish Congress, 45

Xi Jinping, 82, 148, 160

Yanukovych, Viktor, xviii, 16–19
  national dialogue, 20
  flees to Russia, 21
  Putin bribes, 24
Yatsenyuk, Arseniy, 21, 24
Yellen, Janet, 166
Yeltsin, Boris, 9, 36
  hands over to Putin, 37, 149, 153
  sickness, 170
YouTube, 109
Younger, Alex, xxvii
Yukos Oil, xiii, 38
Yurchak, Alexei, 3
Yushchenko, Viktor, 17–18

Zaporizhzhia plant, 84, 86–8, 132
Zelensky, Volodymyr, 27–33
  invasion a shock, 81
  demand for F-16s, 84
  addresses the General Assembly, 120
  swap land for peace deal, 120
  danger of assassination, 153
Zhukov, Georgy, 10
Zuckerberg, Mark, 143